Prentice Hall Guide
To Advanced Communication

Guide to
Electronic Communication

USING TECHNOLOGY FOR EFFECTIVE BUSINESS WRITING AND SPEAKING

Kristen Bell DeTienne
Marriott School of Management
Brigham Young University

PRENTICE HALL
Upper Saddle River, New Jersey 07458

To David, Michael, and Elizabeth
To be blessed with such a wonderful family is truly a gift from God.

Library of Congress Cataloging-in-Publication Data
DeTienne, Kristen Bell.
   Guide to electronic communication : using technology for effective business writing
and speaking / by Kristen Bell DeTienne.
      p. cm.
   Includes bibliographical references and index.
   ISBN 0-13-093348-1
      1. Business communication—Technological innovations. 2. Business
writing—Technological innovations. 3. Business presentations—Technological
innovations. I. Title: Electronic communication. II. Title.

HF5718 .D47 2001
658.4'5—dc21   2001021998

Editor-in-Chief: Jeff Shelstad
Assistant Editor: Jennifer Surich
Editorial Assistant:
  Virginia Sheridan
Media Project Manager:
  Michele Faranda
Senior Marketing Manager:
  Debbie Clare
Marketing Assistant: Brian Rappelfeld
Managing Editor (Production):
  Judy Leale
Production Editor: Theresa Festa
Production Assistant: Keri Jean
Permissions Coordinator:
  Suzanne Grappi

Associate Director, Manufacturing:
  Vincent Scelta
Production Manager: Arnold Vila
Design Manager: Patricia Smythe
Designer: Steve Frim
Art Director: Jayne Conte
Cover Design: Kiwi Design
Associate Director, Multimedia
  Production: Karen Goldsmith
Manager, Print Production:
  Christy Mahon
Composition: Rainbow Graphics
Full-Service Project Management:
  Rainbow Graphics
Printer/Binder: Victor Graphics, Inc.

Credits and acknowledgements borrowed from other sources and reproduced, with
permission, in this textbook appear on appropriate page within text.

10 9 8 7 6 5 4 3
ISBN 0-13-093348-1

Table of Contents

CHAPTER V

ELECTRONIC TOOLS FOR
ORAL COMMUNICATION

CHAPTER VI

ELECTRONIC TOOLS FOR JOB SEARCHES

Introduction

HOW THIS BOOK CAN HELP YOU

If you have ever wondered how to handle all of the emails you receive, how to find the information you're looking for on the web, or how to use up-to-date visual aids to be a more effective speaker, then this book is for you. As skilled as you are in most aspects of your life, you may be uncomfortable with some aspects of new technologies or unaware of some of the powerful new technologies available. This book is designed to give you an edge every time you use electronic communication technology such as presentation software, email, or the Internet.

Even if you don't have a specific question, this book can help you by providing general guidelines, tips, and techniques for using a variety of forms of electronic communication. For example, would you like suggestions on:

- Designing a powerful slide show to win an important account or contract?
- Utilizing videoconferencing and web conferencing to cut the time you spend traveling?
- Managing all of the email messages you receive every day?
- Distributing multimedia business cards to clients and employees?
- Finding the information you need to make the right decision?
- Understanding how to make the most of chat rooms and newsgroups?
- Using your cell phone without offending those around you?
- Using electronic tools to find the right job?

If you want information about other kinds of communication in a business or management setting, please see the other books in this Prentice Hall series on Advanced Communication. All of the books in this series are short, professional, and readable.

- *Guide to Managerial Communication: Effective Business Writing and Speaking* by Mary Munter (Prentice Hall, 2000).
- *Guide to Meetings* by Mary Munter and Michael Netzley (Prentice Hall, 2002)

v

- *Guide to Presentations* by Mary Munter and Lynn Russell (Prentice Hall, 2002)
- *Guide to Report Writing* by Michael Netzley and Craig Snow (Prentice Hall, 2002)

WHO CAN USE THIS BOOK

If you use electronic communication technology, then this guide is for you. You may be reading this book as part of an executive seminar, an MBA class, or a workshop. The book was written for anyone who wants a concise, professional, readable summary of tips and techniques for effectively using technology to communicate.

WHY THIS BOOK WAS WRITTEN

The thousands of participants in various professional electronic communication courses and workshops I have taught—at Brigham Young University and the University of Southern California business schools, as well as at dozens of companies and organizations—tell me they want a brief summary of electronic communication techniques. Such busy professionals have found other books on this subject too long or too remedial for their needs. That's why Prentice Hall is publishing this series, the Prentice Hall Guides to Advanced Communication—brief, practical, reader-friendly guides for people who communicate in professional contexts. (See the opening page in this book for more information on the series.)

- *Brief:* The book summarizes key ideas only. Culling from thousands of pages of text and research, I have omitted bulky examples, cases, footnotes, exercises, and discussion questions.
- *Practical:* This book offers clear, straightforward tools you can use. It includes only information you will find useful in a professional context.
- *Reader-friendly:* The book provides an easy-to-skim format—using a direct, matter-of-fact, and nontheoretical tone.

HOW THIS BOOK IS ORGANIZED

This book is organized into six chapters.

I. Trends in Electronic Communication

Being an effective communicator involves being aware of how technology affects communication. The first part of this chapter discusses current trends that are affecting electronic communication: the knowledge economy and knowledge management, e-business and the web, and telecommuting and virtual companies. The second part of the chapter reviews the effects of e-communication trends: loss of privacy, future trends, and increased media choice.

II. Electronic Tools for Conducting Research

This chapter provides information about how to use technology to collect and manage information. It covers how to use electronic resources in your research, how intranets and extranets are used, how online surveys are conducted, and how personal digital assistants can help you manage your own personal data and information.

III. Electronic Tools for Written Communication

This section of the book addresses technologies that affect printed and electronically transferred writing. It starts with helpful tips for using technology to improve your writing. Next, the chapter offers guidelines for using email, sending faxes, participating in electronic discussion forums, and utilizing multimedia business cards.

IV. Designing Web Pages

The fourth chapter of this book examines one of the fastest-growing areas of e-communication: web design. First, the chapter discusses setting your strategy. Second, it provides guidelines for planning and designing a web site. Third, the chapter offers suggestions for managing a web site.

V. Electronic Tools for Oral Communication

This chapter offers techniques for successfully using electronic media when communicating orally. It includes tips for using electronic presentation aids, electronic conferencing, and telephones.

VI. Electronic Tools for Job Searches

Chapter 6 offers suggestions for using technology in your job search. The chapter describes techniques for designing and distributing an electronic résumé and ways to use the web in your job search.

E–Glossary

The final section of this book defines commonly used electronic communication terms. Throughout the book, potentially confusing words are bolded and italicized. These words, along with selected other terms, are defined using everyday language in the glossary.

ACKNOWLEDGMENTS

A great deal of the information in this book is a result of conversations I have had with colleagues and students at Brigham Young University and businesspersons I've had the pleasure of working with. Thank you for all you've taught me. Special thanks to my colleagues Bill Baker, Michael Thompson, Garth Hanson, Kaye Hanson, Karl Smart, and Karen Lewis Papka who edited drafts of this book. I also appreciate the counsel I've received from my colleagues in the Management Communication Association.

My research assistants, Louise Nickelson and Holly Cornia, provided significant input into this book. They gathered current research, analyzed its applicability, and helped me put together the ideas. Melissa Leilani Larson helped with word processing. Professor Mary Munter critiqued early and penultimate drafts of this guide and offered valuable feedback.

Special thanks to David, Michael, and Elizabeth for their constant support and encouragement.

Kristen Bell DeTienne
Marriott School of Management
Brigham Young University

CHAPTER I OUTLINE

I. E-COMMUNICATION TRENDS
1. Knowledge economy and knowledge management
2. E-business and the Web
3. Telecommuting and virtual companies

II. COMMUNICATION EFFECTS OF E-COMMUNICATION
1. Loss of privacy
2. Future trends
3. Increased media choice

CHAPTER I

Trends in Electronic Communication

Electronic aspects of business communication are changing rapidly, to say the least. This book examines the ways in which this technology can be used to help people create, send, and receive messages. This book is about e-communication.

E-communication is a term used to describe human communication that is assisted by some type of advanced technology. Examples of e-communication are email and *streaming audio.* The focus of this book, then, is to discuss when and how technology can and should be used for communication, not on how the technology works.

The first part of this chapter provides an overview of trends in electronic communication (e-communication): knowledge economy and knowledge management, *e-business* and the web, and telecommuting and virtual companies. The second part of the chapter examines the effects of current trends: loss of privacy, future changes, and increased media choice.

Throughout the book, potentially confusing terms are set in bold italics and defined in the E–Glossary, pages 102–111.

I. E-COMMUNICATION TRENDS

This section introduces some of the major reasons why e-communication is increasing. The ever-increasing pace of change makes current knowledge obsolete very quickly, thus increasing the need for effective communication and knowledge transfer. The following three trends have affected the increasing amount of and need for electronic communication.

1. Knowledge economy and knowledge management

Most experts agree that what is driving the economy is not information but information plus knowledge put to use. As Peter Drucker points out, knowledge workers are the emerging dominant group in what is called the *knowledge economy.* According to the Ministry of Economic Development, over 60 percent of U.S. workers are knowledge workers. In every free-market developed country, industrial workers do not account for more than one-eighth of the workforce and farmers do not account for more than one-twentieth of the workforce. The U.S. economy is called a knowledge economy because it is driven by knowledge, not by industrial products, and because the majority of workers are knowledge workers.

Today, the dominant competitive factor is how well the person, company, industry, or country performs in acquiring, disseminating, sharing, and applying knowledge. Efficient knowledge transfer leads to higher-quality products and services through application of best practices throughout an organization. It also facilitates a company's ability to innovate and change quickly.

The basic goal of "knowledge management" is to leverage and reuse knowledge resources to achieve a competitive advantage and to improve the bottom line. Businesses want to help employees to transfer best practices, based on prior experience the company has, rather than wasting time repeatedly reinventing the wheel. Companies want to use prior knowledge to reduce product development time. Organizations also want to avoid losing large amounts of information and knowledge due to employee turnover.

In a 1999 study by the Conference Board, 82 percent of leading companies surveyed said they were engaged in knowledge management activities; furthermore, 97 percent of the respondents said their companies would be involved in knowledge management within the next five years. Research shows that a growing number of companies are showing large savings, as well as improved performance, by implementing new ways for employees to create and share knowledge. The knowledge economy and knowledge management has led to the following business communication trends:

- *Managers are now responsible* for making knowledge productive, not for producing products.
- *Informal groups,* known as "communities of practice," will be valued by companies for their ability to share tacit knowledge.
- *Employees are increasingly being made part* of the company's governing process.
- *Life-long learning* is essential for keeping pace with change.
- *Knowledge of facts* is not as important as knowledge of people and social processes.
- *Information and communication* technologies are important facilitators of knowledge creation and sharing.

In the knowledge age, your ability to effectively use electronic communication technologies will directly impact your success at work.

2. E-business and the Web

Since 1995, when the ***World Wide Web*** (also called the Web or Internet) came into general use, business communication has changed dramatically and will continue to do so. Every 100 days, web traffic doubles. In 1999, only about 250 million people used the web. However, experts predict as many as one billion people will use the web by 2005. The web has led to (1) a new way to buy and sell products and services, called *electronic commerce* (or ***e-commerce***) and (2) a new way to conduct business and exchange information, called ***e-business.*** The following list provides examples of the changes being introduced by the web and e-business:

- *Decreasing face-to-face communication:* Consumers no longer have to interact with sales persons to buy products.
- *Easier access to information:* Buyers can easily compare prices on the

same product. Customers can use the web to find accurate, up-to-date information and price comparisons.

- *More anonymity:* The anonymity of the web reduces the impact of personality.

- *New business opportunities:* Increasing numbers of companies are emerging that offer products and services that facilitate electronic communication—web design, editing, consulting, and electronic bill pay services—entirely online. For instance, the number of **search engines,** directories, and remote surveillance companies has exploded.

- *New work flows:* In addition, e-business has led to entirely new work flows. For example, employees often don't have to drive to a library to obtain the information they need (they search the web); writers don't have to deliver hard copies of their work to print shops (they instantly send electronic copies directly to readers); managers do not have to call to ask about inventory levels (they obtain accurate counts via an **extranet**).

Because these trends are reducing the impact of personality, business communication is more important than ever. Clear writing, accurate information, and effective presentation are crucial to success in today's world.

3. Telecommuting and virtual companies

Electronic communication technology—including email, voice mail, cell phones, and **web conferencing**—has enabled people to **telecommute;** that is, work at home, connected only electronically to the office. Nearly twenty percent of the American workforce telecommutes. Studies show that employees who telecommute are often 10 to 20 percent more productive than employees who do not.

Kind of jobs   Telecommuters may work at a wide range of jobs:

- *Financial management:* Financial planners meet with clients in their homes and offices but perform most of the financial management activities such as trading stocks and developing balanced portfolios from their homes.

- *Computer programming and engineering:* Engineers and programmers compose software programs on their computers at home.

- *Consulting:* Experts travel to clients' offices to gather information and consult with executives and work at home when conducting analysis, writing reports, and the like.

- *Writing, word processing, and transcription:* Documents, ***web pages,*** and email messages are composed or typed at home and can be sent to the office electronically.
- *Answering phones:* Calls are routed to the employee's home phone. Employees can take orders, provide assistance, and perform customer service duties.
- *Monitoring:* Many processes, such as computer networks, security operations, and sales reports can be monitored using an Internet connection from home.
- *Education:* Many classes and homework assignments can be completed electronically.

Kinds of telecommuting   When all of the employees in a company telecommute, and no bricks-and-mortar building exists, the company is known as a *"virtual company"* (or *cyberorganization*). When all the members of a team or work group within a bricks-and-mortar company telecommute, they are known as a *virtual team* or *virtual group.* Finally, since almost half of American businesses offer employees some type of flexible scheduling, probably many other individuals are telecommuting part time.

II. COMMUNICATION EFFECTS OF E-COMMUNICATION

The fast pace of change, including the e-communication trends just discussed, results in other communication-related outcomes. The major effects are discussed in the following sections, the first of which is a loss of privacy.

1. Loss of privacy

One of the most important effects of the recent technological changes is a loss of privacy. Privacy is an issue that affects everyone at an individual level. As a consumer, protect your personal information; avoid the "it won't happen to me" syndrome. As an employee, find out what your company's policy is; do not use your company's electronic equipment for personal business, such as sending personal email, web *surf-*

ing, or word processing. As a manager, be sensitive to your employees' needs for privacy; listen to their concerns.

Privacy issues must also be examined from an organizational level. Protecting employee and customer privacy is as important as protecting payroll data and company secrets. If your customers do not trust your site, they will do business with companies they trust. If your employees do not trust you with their personal information, they will leave to work for companies they do trust.

Consider these privacy considerations from the perspective of a consumer, employee, and manager.

Consumer privacy issues   As a consumer, you do have some control over your private information. Research shows that nearly 90 percent of Americans on the Web worry about businesses and strangers obtaining personal information about them. However, the same study found that fewer than 10 percent of users take precautions while they surf! The following tips will help you protect your own privacy online:

- *Read the privacy policies* on the web sites you use.
- *Look for privacy seals* (e.g., TRUSTe, BBBOnline) and verify their authenticity.
- *Safeguard private information* such as your **passwords.**
- *Block* **cookies** that carry your private information to unknown sources. Most browsers contain features that allow you to reject cookies. Also, www.junkbusters.com offers a free program that blocks cookies and unwanted banner ads.
- *Ensure you have a secure connection* (e.g., **SSL, SET**) when communicating private information online.
- *Use* **encryption** *software* (e.g., **PGP, FTP.SSH,** SFTP, **HTTPS**) when transferring sensitive information.
- *Register with an* **infomediary,** such as iPrivacy, that will protect you from disclosing sensitive information to a questionable source.

Employee privacy issues   Do not expect any privacy as an employee at work. From a legal standpoint, most cases have supported an employer's right to monitor employees doing their work. These rights generally extend as far as giving employers the right to listen in on work calls, read employees' email messages, and monitor their whereabouts.

In fact, a 2000 study of 2,133 companies conducted by the American Management Association revealed that over 73 percent of businesses admit to spying on employees electronically. A word to the wise is to assume your boss can see, hear, and read all of your communications at work, employment related or not.

Managerial privacy issues   If you are a manager at work, your employees' privacy will be a major issue for you. The following tips will familiarize you with some of the issues involved in developing a privacy policy:

- *Talk to your company's lawyer first.* Find out what laws and regulations your company should be following in each of the locations you do business. Know the rules first.

- *Assess your company's current practices.* What data is being collected, by which divisions, for what reasons? What is being done with the information? Who has access to it? Did the company have permission to collect it? What do the employees and customers know about and feel about the company's privacy practices? Does your company have the necessary firewalls in place?

- *Evaluate your company's strengths and weaknesses,* risks and opportunities. Write a policy that is clear and fair. Solicit input and feedback from many sources. Consult helpful companies and web sites (such as www.eff.org, www.epic.org, and www.privacybot.com).

- *Talk to your company's lawyer again.* Review the privacy policy and make changes necessary to stay in compliance with all rules and laws.

- *Communicate the new policy* using several communication channels: orally, in writing, and electronically. Clarify expectations. Post the policy on your company's web site and in the meeting rooms, information systems department, Chief Knowledge Officer's (CKO) office, and human resources offices.

- *Periodically audit the entire organization* to ensure compliance with the written policy. Update the policy to keep pace with changing public opinion and new laws.

2. Future trends

In addition to the specific trends we have already witnessed, additional other factors will affect electronic communication in the future. These changes point to the increased use of technology in communication.

- *Interactivity:* We will see an increase in the amount of two-way communication; we will be able to send messages and solicit feedback with increasing frequency and ease.

- *Mobility:* We will be able to communicate more from remote locations. Through the use of satellite cell phones, DSL (Digital Subscriber Lines), and other technology, individuals will have increased opportunities to communicate while away from home and work.

- *Convertibility:* We will easily transform spoken messages to written and written documents into spoken words. We will be able to convert visual, auditory, and sensory signals to other signals and formats.

- *Connectivity:* We will have an easier time using technology. Manufacturers of communications equipment are striving to make the technologies compatible. Increasingly, we will be able to connect equipment and use standard protocols to transfer information.

- *Ubiquity:* We will have access to more technology in more places. Increasing numbers of people will have access to electronic communication media regardless of their socioeconomic level.

- *Globalization:* We will see blurring cultural boundaries. Information and knowledge will spread worldwide. Innovative technology will provide new avenues for international communication between and within companies.

3. Increased media choice

Another effect of electronic communication has to do with the increasing variety of media through which people communicate. Years ago, the two communication media were writing and speaking. Today, communication media includes fax, email, voice mail, electronic meetings, videoconferencing, and more.

Every time you communicate, you choose what medium to use. All too often, this choice is made unconsciously, especially when using common electronic media such as telephones or email. Each kind of technology offers unique benefits and drawbacks that change depending on the audience, purpose, and cost.

Push technology   When making choices about which technology to use, you'll want to consider whether push technology or pull technology is a better approach. Push technology gives all employees all of the information, whether they need it or not. Pushing, such as sending an email to all employees, can work well in instances when every-one must have the information. However, the result is often informa-tion overload.

Pull technology   On the other hand, pull technology makes all of the information available, so that employees can pull out what they need. This there-when-you-need-it approach, such as a corporate *intranet,* works well when you're not sure which employee will need which information. In addition to your decision to use push versus pull technology, you must consider the importance of nonverbal aspects of communication.

Nonverbal considerations   Beware of overdependence and overre-liance on technology that filters out nonverbal aspects of communi-cation. When we use telephones, email, fax, intranets, and other forms of electronic communication, we don't always know the age, status, mood, or gender of the receiver. Without this information, we may be more likely to be disorganized, insensitive, and abrupt.

Each individual section of this book looks at when to use and when not to use a particular media. In addition, the first chapter of *The Guide to Managerial Communication* (GMC) lists the advantages and disadvantages of various electronic media. This information, cou-pled with the information you have about your particular audience and purpose, will help you make quality choices about which tech-nology to use in any situation.

Knowing about the trends discussed in this chapter will help you understand how communication is changing, and why electronic com-munication skills are increasingly important at work. Since electronic communication is so prevalent and so important, the following chap-ters will offer helpful information for effectively using technology to communicate.

CHAPTER 2 OUTLINE

I. CONDUCTING ELECTRONIC SEARCHES
1. Using web search tools
2. Using business sites
3. Choosing keywords or terms
4. Finding and verifying credible sources

II. USING ELECTRONIC DATABASES

III. USING OTHER ELECTRONIC SOURCES
1. Intranets and extranets
2. Online surveys
3. Personal digital assistants

CHAPTER 2

Electronic Tools for Conducting Research

In business, it is not always "what you know" that counts. No one can know everything. Often, it's "what you can find out" that makes you effective at work. Therefore, knowing how to efficiently find the information you need can help you and your company make the right decisions.

Data collection and management are important for knowledge management. Many years ago, companies enjoyed competitive advantages through production efficiencies. In the last two decades, we have watched the transition from the production economy to the information economy. Experts predict that we are now entering a knowledge economy in which a competitive advantage will be based on the efficient and effective management of knowledge within a company. How is this done? Through communication.

To be competitive, companies must be able to collect and manage information efficiently and effectively. Many web sites provide helpful advice about finding information on the Internet. For example, see www.notess.com/search, http://searchenginewatch.com, and http://lib.berkeley.edu/TeachingLib/Guides/Internet/FindInfo.html

The purpose of this chapter is to provide concise information about data collection and management in the areas of (1) electronic searches, (2) electronic databases, and (3) other electronic tools (intranets and extranets, online surveys, and personal digital assistants).

I. CONDUCTING ELECTRONIC SEARCHES

By now, you're probably very familiar with the World Wide Web. Perhaps you've bought items at an online auction or purchased movie tickets or read restaurant reviews. You may have tracked stocks and bonds, found company financial information, or researched specific information for classwork. If so, you know that an amazing amount of information is available on the web. But finding the exact information you want can be difficult. If you haven't already deciphered the intricacies of web searching, here are some suggestions for finding quality business information that will help you keep up with what's happening in the business world at large and will help you perform well in your job. This section will describe how to conduct an electronic search and how to find and verify credible sources.

1. Using web search tools

You may wonder what information is available on the web that may be helpful to you in your job or business. The answer is almost anything! You can get investment advice, track stock performance, read company financial statements or relevant articles, find consultants in many fields, use library databases, access government records, and get help with web design as well as locate resources for creating *web pages.*

The most commonly used tools for searching the web are directories, *search engines,* and multiple search engines. Another alternative is to go to an expert advice web site. The following sections will describe each tool and will provide web site addresses for examples of each.

To use a search directory or engine, go to the home page and simply click on the business section or whatever area you're interested in. Then follow the *links* to the specific area you want to research. At any given point you can opt to use the search function instead of following directory links. The search function will provide results for directories and for individual sites. Whether you are using a directory or a search engine, you must delimit your search effectively.

Directories are used for specific searches. They return more relevant responses as well as more professional sites.

- Yahoo! (www.yahoo.com) is smaller and more discriminatory than other directories and thus is faster. It's good for mainstream information or requests and has good business links.

- Galaxy (www.galaxy.com) tries to cover many topics and thus, has little depth, but it has excellent links in the business section.

- Excite (www.excite.com) provides a quality subject directory with business categories and business links such as stock and company performance.

- InfoSeek (www.go.com) is a commercial search engine with a large following and so is busy. It's geared toward commercial users and has a large commercial database and quick response time.

- Madalyn (www.udel.edu/alex/mba/main/netdir2.html) is a site maintained by the University of Delaware MBA program with links to all areas of business.

Search engines generally provide more responses than directories. Search engines are the first choice for most people for web searching, but they tend to return too many responses, many of them irrelevant, especially if you're looking for business information.

- AltaVista (www.altavista.digital.com) is a good search engine that has features for sophisticated searching using proximity terms and abbreviations.

- Google (www.google.com) is simple and fast but returns so many results it's effective only if you can use narrow search terms.

- Hotbot (www.hotbot.com) is a large index and a good place to search for unusual topics or using unusual search terms. It provides good advanced search options.

Multiple search engines perform the most exhaustive searches. Multiple search engines are an excellent source when you want a comprehensive web search because they use several different search engines in their search. However, like search engines, most of the responses are likely to be commercial sites.

- Dogpile (www.dogpile.com) searches 20 engines, three at a time. This approach can save you time when you need a broad-based search.

- Metacrawler (www.metacrawler.com) searches multiple directories quickly.

Expert advice sites try to answer any question you might have. Many give you an open field in which you can type in any question. Beware, however, as many are slanted toward answering buying questions. According to Bovee and Thill's October 2000 newsletter, the top expert advice web sites are the following:

- *www.askjeeves.com:* Offers fast and free automated advice. The computer picks up on key words in your questions; thus, answers do not necessarily respond to your exact question.

- *www.abuzz.com:* Requires you to register in order to have a question answered.

- *www.askme.com:* Allows you to ask any question and can give specific advice, but it requires you to wait for an email response to your query.

- *www.exp.com:* Contracts with real experts to answer your questions. There is a charge for the assistance, which varies according to the experience and education of the person you ask to help.

- *www.askanything.com:* Insists that you sign up before you can get help. Uses a bid pricing system to charge you for assistance.

- *www.inforocket.com:* Charges a fee; answers your questions using a human. The answerer gets 80 percent of the fee and Inforocket gets 20 percent of the fee.

- *www.webhelp.com:* Uses a live person to respond to your query. You get your free answer online while you wait (5 to 20 minutes) and the transcript of the conversation is sent to the email address you must give.

- *www.soyouwanna.com:* Provides a variety of topics from which you choose. Does not allow you to type in a question. Offers free Internet access.

- *www.expertcentral.com:* Uses human volunteers to answer your question for free.

- *www.xcelco.on.ca/~johnston/know.html:* Contains links to over 900 expert advice sites covering a wide range of topics.

Web research sites provide organized links to research sources. Most are free and easy to use. According to the November 2000 Business Communication Update, the top eight web research sites are the following:

- *www.bigchalk.com:* Allows you to search by keyword or subject. Geared toward students.

- *www.clearinghouse.net:* Offers links to virtual libraries, Internet directories, and Internet search tools.
- *www.ehow.com:* Provides 15,000 step-by-step how-tos; allows you to search using natural language or categories. Free newsletter.
- *www.elibrary.com:* Allows you to search the web for newspaper articles, magazine articles, books, television and radio transcripts, maps, and other sources.
- *www.infoplease.com:* Provides various research tools including a dictionary, almanac, atlas, or encyclopedia.
- *www.itools.com:* Allows you to search by largest web sites, best results, or categorized results, using Yahoo!, Alta Vista, GO Network, Northern Light, and other links.
- *www.learn2.com:* Is aimed toward businesses and features thousands of commercial products and services.
- *www.refdesk.com:* Contains links to thousands of sites, including areas of statistics, journalism, encyclopedias, and current events.

2. Using business sites

In addition to going to general engines, you can go to specific sites to find business information. Many business-oriented sites offer memberships or affiliation, some for a fee and others for free. For example, at Brint.com, you can join the BizTech Network—it's free—and one benefit is their newsletter. The newsletter has a list of recent articles and *URLs* to get to the full-text article, announcements of conferences, book publications, sales, and job openings. These same sites often offer a personalized home page: you specify what kinds of information you're interested in, and the site automatically puts it on your page. The following sections describe major business information directories and sites.

Business information directories   Various directories are available on the web that are geared to business needs. The list below contains several good sites that are themselves directories, with a wide array of information and links.

- *Brint.com (www.brint.com):* A *metasite* that calls itself the "Internet Business Technology Portal" and has links to directories of many kinds, newswires, journals and magazines, company and industry information.

- *Business.com (www. business.com):* Claims to offer "organized business information without the clutter" and has links to articles from sources like the *Wall Street Journal* or by well-known authors in the field, to research sources, and to business web sites.

- *Hoover's Online (www.hoovers.com):* Another very large site with company information, from performance rankings to financial data, sections on money, career development, news, business travel, and a purchasing center for business-related items.

- *Inc.com (www.Inc.com):* Geared especially toward small businesses.

- *Smartbiz.com (www.Smartbiz.com):* Has a good database—good for specific requests, harder to browse.

- *FindArticles.com (www.findarticles.com):* Offers free full-text articles from over 300 reputable magazines and journals in a variety of fields.

Other business information sites   Other places to check for business information on the web are the web sites of business journals and magazines, newspapers, and business associations, and company *web sites*. The URLs for examples of these types of sites are listed below. Also, most major companies have sites.

- *Journals and magazines*
  www.businessweek.com
  www.fortune.com
  www.forbes.com
  www.industryweek.com

- *Newspapers*
  www.wallstreetjournal.com or www.wsj.com
  www.financialtimes.com or www.ft.com
  www.nytimes.com

- *Business associations*
  www.informs.org (the Institute for Operations Research and the Management Sciences site contains links to dozens of other professional association sites)
  www.aom.pace.edu (Academy of Management)
  www.decisionsciences.org (Decision Sciences Institute)
  www.aaa-edu.org (American Accounting Association)
  www.ipl.org/ref/AON (lists over 2,000 Internet sites providing information on professional and trade associations)

- *Government sites*
  www.cbdnet.gpo.gov (Commerce Business Daily): Updated every day;

gives information about hundreds of ways to get money out of the U.S. government.
www.sba.gov (Small Business Administration): Provides information about starting a small business, small business loans, etc.
www.irs.gov (Internal Revenue Service): Contains specific information about tax rules and regulations.

- *Think tanks*
www.heritage.org: Engages in political discussions
www.stncar.com: Promotes future transportation solutions

- *National phone books/Personal contact information sites* help you to easily locate colleagues and friends
www.555-1212.com
www.anywho.com
www.bigfoot.com

If you know the name of a specific company or periodical, you can often find the web page simply by typing in www.(company or periodical name).com. For example, you can type www.ibm.com or www.gm.com or www.microsoft.com or www.bain.com. Finding the web page this way may be faster than using a search engine. Beware, however—sometimes other companies "cyber squat" on a well-known business name. If you type www.(company).com and do not find the site you are looking for, just go to a directory or engine and use the company name as your search term. Once you've found the information you want, you will need to determine how useful that information is.

3. Choosing keywords or terms

When searching, you need to structure your search through the words or terms you choose to use. If the search term is too broad, you can get thousands of *hits* and if the terms are too narrow, you can miss the very item you're looking for. Research has shown that search engines provide the right information less than 40 percent of the time. The following tips can help you delimit your search effectively and increase your success rate.

- *Use a search engine or directory* that has advanced search options that allow you to use *Boolean operators,* specify what's on the pages, find or reject sites associated with certain words or phrases, and search within the results of a broad search. Read the directions on the site (usually under a tab labeled "advanced search") to understand your search options. The more specific you can make your search, the more likely you will be to find what you want and exclude what you don't want. (See MSN example on page 21.)

- *Follow the links* to the area of business you're interested in within the directory or search engine. Then try a search using moderately narrow terms.

- *Look at the descriptions of the first few responses.* If they aren't what you want, look for commonalities that can help you delimit your search further.

- *Use quotation marks around a phrase to help narrow your search.* Quotation marks tell the search engine to look for a phrase rather than separate words, and can help to narrow your search. For example, a search asking for John Doe would find sites with John or Doe. "John Doe" would just find sites with the full name.

- *Pick out one or two terms* that are associated with irrelevant responses and put them in as "Should not contain" or "Not near" and try again. Some search engines use negative signs; "heart - attack" would find sites with heart, but not heart attack.

- *Choose one or two terms* associated with the responses that are relevant and use them as "Should Contain" or "Near."

- *Try broadening your search* by using only part of the terms if you're looking for a site you know is there but can't find. The site may have moved or changed its name. If a site has changed names, you may be able to find it by going to www.lycos.com/cgi-bin/url_finder.cgi

- *Use bookmarks.* As you search, bookmark interesting sites you may want to explore later.

The figure on the next page shows advanced search engine techniques on the topic of videoconferencing using Microsoft's www.msn.com. It has "videoconferencing" + "tips" or "suggestions" – "sales" in the *Search the web for:* box. If the search were just "videoconferencing" it would be too broad. If it included "videoconferencing and tips" it might be too narrow. By including "tips" or "suggestions" it looks for sites that include one or the other. The search ends with – "sales" so it will not include commercial sites that include the word sales. Notice the site also lets you specify the region, language, and other options.

Example: Advanced search techniques

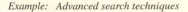

Screen shot reprinted by permission from Microsoft Corporation.

As with any skill, practice helps, so allocate some time to learning to search effectively. Taking the time to read the directions for the engine you're using will probably save you time in the long run. Also, classes and workshops can increase your skills, and you can make use of people you know who can point you to quality sites they have discovered. With some experience, you'll learn where the best sites in your field are and how to find new, high-quality sites.

4. Finding and verifying credible sources

Once you've found information using the techniques described in the previous section, verify that the information is reliable. Find reliable information by going to traditionally reliable sources such as a large company, well-known publisher, research center, think tank, university, government agency, and so on. You can look up information on the author in the *Encyclopedia of Associations* (available at www.silverplatter.com) or the relevant version of *Who's Who*. Another helpful site for determining reliability is www.umuc.edu/library/evaluate.html. You also can use print or online directories to find other articles by the same author.

Determine accuracy   Think about how you plan to use the information to determine how much time you want to spend establishing its credibility. If you must have accurate information, you can verify web site authorship by going to the home page, finding other sources that substantiate the information, and by checking directories of published documents. Ask questions such as: Is the site or publication peer reviewed? Why is the information presented? How does the reason for presenting it affect the likelihood of its accuracy? Are there links to other credible sites?

Check the source and/or authorship   Who wrote the page and why? Is the writer an authority, and does she have obvious biases? Has she footnoted or referenced her sources? Is the source one you can assume is reliable, or can you verify the information some way? Can you find any responses to what has been written? Has she written anything else? The answers to these questions will help you establish the credibility of the author, and thus, the credibility of the information. Is the information from a person, a company, a well-known organization or group, a university? Is more than one view given? Does the site provide a contact person? Does the *domain name* match the stated source?

Examine the web page itself   High-quality sources will have polished, professional-looking pages. Spelling errors and grammatical mistakes should warn you away. What is the publication date? If time sensitive, is the information current?

Document the URL   If you decide the information is useful to you, document the URL and the date for your records. The best way to do this is to print a copy of the information, including the home page of the site. As you become more familiar with a given field, you will be better able to recognize sources, to determine the quality of the information, and to trace or substantiate data. Always make use of your own common sense, too: If it sounds exaggerated or too good to be true, it probably is.

II. USING ELECTRONIC DATABASES

You can find up-to-date, reliable information and ideas in databases designed for business professionals. Database searches have advantages over web searches: The search has already been effectively delimited by subject area and periodical type in the database, and the quality of the sources is generally excellent.

You have probably already used some of these databases. Spend enough time in the library to become familiar with what databases are available, especially in your area of emphasis. You will be a more effective decision maker if you have an idea of the resources available to you.

If the company you work for doesn't have access to databases you want to use, you can pay the relatively small fee to get a card for the nearest university or large library so you can access the databases through that library. In addition, many large libraries have employees who will research for you—anything from the performance of specific companies to the source for an important cite.

Even if you don't have access to a large library, you may find a small, local library very helpful. Today, the majority of libraries are linked by a system that parallels the web. Even small public libraries can access the catalogs of large libraries across the world. Through interlibrary loans, you can get books or periodicals sent to you, often in just a few days for a minimal charge. Libraries tend to be underutilized, so if you know and use library sources, you may have an edge on the competition.

The following lists give you an idea of the variety of databases available. Usually, you need to go to a library and/or pay a fee to use a database over the web.

Multiple subject directories contain listings of directories and resources for multiple subject areas.

- *Lexis/Nexis:* Full-text, multisubject directory emphasizing law, business, current events, including periodicals.
- *Academic Universe:* A condensed form of Lexis/Nexis

Periodical indexes include listings within a specific subject area.

- *ABI Inform:* Contains the most current, dependable articles on business and management, most of them in full text.
- *Consumer Index:* Gives product reviews.
- *Insurance Periodicals:* Indexes periodicals: benefits, casualties, compensation, estates, financial and planning services, etc.
- *Market Center:* Tracks the stock market.
- *National Trade Data Bank:* Contains 90,000 documents and statistical tables about U.S. trade and promotion, import/export policies and data.
- *Public Affairs:* Provides indexes to and abstracts of public affairs information, elected officials, current events, foreign affairs and information from periodicals, government documents, and books.
- *US Census:* Provides population, business patterns, and finance data.

Directories provide specific information within a subject area.

- *American Business Directory:* Gives names and addresses of more than 10 million companies.
- *Company Profiles:* Has public and private company data, contact names, addresses and phone numbers, size, sales volume, business descriptions.
- *Moody's International Company Data:* Provides financial statements and information from 11,000 companies in 100 foreign countries.
- Product Name Finder: Indexes products produced worldwide.

Financial and stock information

- *Disclosure:* Corporate and financial information for over 11,000 corporations with shares traded in the United States.
- *Dun and Bradstreet:* Extensive financial data about American and International companies.
- *EDGAR (Electronic Data Gathering, Analysis, and Retrieval System):* Financial reports of U.S. corporations from reports to Securities and Exchange Commission, annual and quarterly company statements, balance sheets, income statements, security activity, etc.
- *Stock reports for the world:* Worldwide stock performance statistics.

III. USING OTHER ELECTRONIC SOURCES

Thus far, we've looked at conducting electronic searches and using electronic databases. Sometimes, however, the situation calls for different methods of data management. The remainder of this chapter will look at intranets and extranets, online surveys, and personal digital assistants as tools and techniques for information management.

1. Intranets and extranets

An intranet is a computer communications tool used inside of companies. Employees from diverse locations use an intranet to access information, share files, ask questions, brainstorm ideas together, and make decisions. The intranet is available to all employees regardless of the computer platform, *browser,* or kind of network they use because it uses Internet technology such as a Web server, TCP/IP, and *HTML.* Experts predict that five times as many web *servers* will be sold for intranets as will be sold for Internets. Increasing numbers of companies are installing intranets every year.

Advantages of intranets include:

- *Facilitates knowledge management initiatives* and helps companies share best practices throughout the organization.

- *Provides an opportunity for employees* to conveniently share information about clients, customers, procedures, policies, and so on; can break down silos of information.

- *Is available to all employees* all over the world 24 hours a day.

- *Provides the most up-to-date financial figures* and corporate information; all employees can work from the same spreadsheet.

- *Is independent of specific hardware and software requirements* for employees.

- *Keeps company information more secure* since **passwords** are needed to use the intranet and to access sensitive information.

- *Saves money.* Meta Group Inc. conducted a return on investment analysis of intranets. Results indicated that 80 percent of companies enjoyed a positive return on their investment, with a 38 percent average annual return.

- *Reduces time and monetary expenses* by reducing employee travel.

- *Supports efficient work flow* (e.g., files can be transferred instantaneously, and employees in one part of the world can work on a project during the day and other employees can work at night).

- *Cuts paper and photocopy expenses.* Owens Corning has started to conduct most of its internal business using the company's intranet. The company uses the intranet instead of paper for company communications, including new policies and announcements, product information, memos, and company news. The company has eliminated 50 percent of its copiers and printers, and 60 percent of its fax machines. Owens Corning has saved $30 to $50 million a year by using its intranet this way.

The drawbacks of intranets include:

- *Can be expensive* to develop a large intranet.

- *Employees can be stressed by information overload* if sent too many messages.

- *Information can be hard to find* if not organized effectively.

- *The system can crash,* leaving employees less productive.

- *Employees can accidentally post sensitive information.*

To see an example of an intranet, and to find links to other sites with intranet information, go to www.intrack.com/intranet/demo.shtml

Extranets   An extranet is like an intranet, except that it is available for people outside the company, too. A company uses an extranet to communicate with suppliers, customers, and others who directly impact the company's production, operations, and marketing. Again, passwords are used to maintain security of the information.

Most of the advantages and disadvantages are the same for extranets as for intranets. They facilitate timely, accurate communication between companies. Extranets can also help companies cut costs. For example, Merisel, Inc., in El Segundo, California, has found that it is 70 percent cheaper to use their extranet to process a customer order than to have an employee handle the order via telephone.

Chrysler provides another example of how extranets can help companies save money. In the mid-1990s, the auto manufacturer realized it would benefit by using the expertise of its suppliers to find ways to improve parts design and production. Chrysler also wanted to be able to rapidly collect and evaluate proposals from thousands of international suppliers. To accomplish these goals, Chrysler installed an extranet. In 1997, the savings was 1.2 billion (yes, billion) due to improved margins. The total savings exceeded 2.5 billion. Intranets and extranets can also be used to conduct online surveys.

2. Online surveys

Another method for gathering useful information is through online surveys. Online surveys are like traditional paper questionnaires except the survey is administered electronically and the responses are collected online. They can be conducted internally, within an organization, or externally by an independent organization. Online surveys are increasingly taking the place of paper-and-pencil surveys because of the cost savings associated with delivering and administering the survey electronically, and automatically inputting the responses and calculating the results.

Uses   Surveys can be collected from employees to determine their feelings and knowledge on a variety of topics. Surveys can be given to customers to ask about their reactions to your products and services.

Surveys can also be used in conjunction with performance appraisals. An increasing number of companies are using 360° surveys to gather employee performance information from a variety of sources such as peers, superiors, subordinates, and customers. A survey by *HR Magazine* found that 90 percent of *Fortune* 100 companies use multisource assessments. Online 360° surveys are a quick, efficient, confidential way for large companies to collect feedback from and distribute feedback to employees.

Advantages and disadvantages   An example from Advanced Micro Devices (AMD) in Sunnyvale, California, helps illustrate some of the advantages. AMD started using online surveys several years ago. It found that when compared to paper surveys, online surveys were less expensive, faster to collect and analyze, more convenient, and more effective at soliciting honest responses. The biggest disadvantage of online surveys is that they can be expensive and time consuming to buy or develop.

3. Personal digital assistants

Personal digital assistants (PDAs) use technology for data management of personal information. Among the top-selling electronic items, these "palm-sized" minicomputers started as digitized organizers, but as with other computer products, each new version has some added capabilities. PDAs not only keep track of appointments, addresses, phone numbers, and financial records, they also can transfer information to or receive information from your desktop computer, track your time and stock trades, display graphics, calculate loans, and perform a wide variety of other specialized tasks. Handwriting recognition software allows you to take notes in longhand, and, of course, you can play games. One of the greatest benefits is that the PDAs are programmable, so you can personalize the PDA to suit your requirements.

The newest PDAs (at this writing) can beam information to each other, provide wireless Internet access, and act as pages. According to a 2000 study by NPD Intellect, Palms accounted for 65 percent and Handspring accounted for 22 percent of the PDAs sold. Other companies that sell PDAs include Casio and Hewlett-Packard. By the time this book is published, other, more specialized hardware and software is sure to be available.

If you don't already own a PDA, think carefully before purchasing one. Consider the tasks you do, the ways you use your desktop and/or laptop computer, and decide what advantages a PDA would offer you. Below are some questions you can ask yourself to help you determine whether purchasing a PDA is a wise choice.

Do you have a large number of appointments or does your schedule change frequently?   People in these situations find the PDA's capability of moving information from and to their main computer saves them time and aggravation. The small size of many units is also a benefit for this group of individuals, who like to carry their PDAs in suit or shirt pockets.

Do you take handwritten notes the PDA can transfer to other records?   This function will then save you considerable time and be convenient.

How often do you need a laptop computer with you?   If a PDA can often supply all the functions you need, you'll prefer the small size as well as the cost savings. PDAs range in weight from 1.41 lbs to 5.7 ounces and may run 2 to 4 weeks on just 2 AAA batteries.

What do you want a PDA to do?   Decide what tasks you're interested in and then research the various models to discover what models will fill your requirements before you narrow your choices.

How much are you willing to spend?   If the model that matches the tasks you want your PDA to perform is expensive, you may be better off with a laptop or minicomputer, which will perform more tasks. Or you may want to revise your ideas, buy an inexpensive PDA that performs basic tasks, and use your main computer for more complex tasks.

If you decide you definitely want a PDA and you know what you want it to be able to do, check out product information and performance reviews on the Internet. When you have narrowed the field to a few models, go to a store (even if you plan on purchasing your PDA over the Internet) and try out several models. You want a unit that not only performs the necessary functions and is in your price range, but also one that feels good to you, that you'll enjoy using. Then search out the best deal on that unit and get organizing!

The information in this chapter will help you to gather and organize the data you need to be effective and to make good decisions at work.

CHAPTER 3 OUTLINE

I TRADITIONAL WRITING
  1. Techniques to help you write faster
  2. Techniques to help you write more effectively

II. EMAIL
  1. When to use email
  2. How to use effective reader access techniques
  3. How to write audience-focused messages
  4. How to send email
  5. How to manage the email you receive

III. FAXES
  1. When to fax
  2. How to fax

IV. ELECTRONIC DISCUSSION FORUMS
  1. How to access sequential discussion forums
  2. How to access real-time discussion forums
  3. How to participate in electronic discussion forums

V. MULTIMEDIA BUSINESS CARDS

CHAPTER 3

Electronic Tools for Written Communication

T echnology is more important now than it ever has been in helping business writers to be effective. This chapter begins by describing several ways in which you can use technology to be a more efficient and effective writer. The following sections explore specific written communication genres—including (1) traditional writing, (2) email, (3) faxes, (4) electronic discussion forums, and (5) multimedia business cards.

I. TRADITIONAL WRITING

You can use software technology in many ways to strengthen your written documents faster and more effectively.

1. Techniques to help you write faster

Computers can help you write faster.

Avoid writer's block   Computers make it simple to brainstorm ideas, knowing it is easy to change or delete unwanted text.

1. Start by quickly typing a vertical brainstormed list.
2. Arrange items by category.
3. Arrange categories into proper sequence; use outlining feature of your computer.
4. Write from this outline, adding introduction and conclusion.

Use boilerplates and mail merge to save time

- *Boilerplate:* When you need to use some of the same content in several documents, you can draft the information once and copy it into all of the documents. Save paragraphs as separate files, or if you use them frequently, set them up as macros (automatic functions) in your word processing program. If you want to send the same written message to many readers, you can compose a carefully worded form letter for all.

- *Mail merge:* Most word processors are equipped with a mail merge feature for names, addresses, salutations, collection amounts, and other individualized content. Mail merge works in conjunction with a database file and automatically inserts unique information into each letter, such as name, address, and collection amount.

2. Techniques to help you write more effectively

Special features of your software programs can also help you be a more effective writer.

Outlining/headings   The outlining feature will help you keep track of your document structure, format the same level of headings in the same font size and style, and make an automatic table of contents from your headings.

Cut and paste   Use cut and paste to move text so your ideas flow better. For example, you may start by unorganized brainstorming, and then add categories and cut and paste the items you brainstormed into the correct categories. Similarly, you might find an ineffective sentence order in the first draft of a paragraph; you can easily cut the topic sentence out of the middle of a paragraph and paste it to be the first sentence.

Microediting   Word processors have many features to help you improve important documents. For example, you can search for expletive constructions (e.g., false subjects such as *it* and *there*) and words you want to replace. If you have been criticized in the past for using certain words (e.g., "a lot") in your writing, you can search for those words and replace them with more descriptive terms.

Footnotes, page numbers, etc   Use the footnoting feature to automatically renumber and reformat your footnotes and endnotes.

Tools (thesaurus, spell check, grammar check)   Open the thesaurus to find the exact word that conveys your meaning. Always pay attention to the words underlined by the spell checker. Use a grammar checker to strengthen your writing. Grammar checkers cannot tell you whether you are communicating clearly or persuasively. However, they can help you with other possible problems, such as pointing out when you are using passive voice, repeated words, overly long sentences, subjects and verbs that don't agree, inappropriate subjunctive mood, and potentially incorrect word choice.

Sounds, pictures, and videos   By using presentation/slideshow software, graphics software, special email programs, and hot links and web links in your word processing documents, you can add life to your documents with background music and sounds, color pictures, and even full motion video clips. Use sounds to emphasize points, add interest, and clarify points. For example, a video capture or sound clip might convey the sound of a certain mechanical failure better than you could in words. When adding hot links, type the whole URL including the http://www, to enable the link in the electronic copy of your document. Of course, you should always consider your audience and the situation when deciding what to include.

II. EMAIL

Studies show that U.S. businesses rely heavily on email: 100 million workers send more than one billion email messages every day. Researchers estimate that by 2002, eight billion email messages will be sent every day. This section will give you tips on when and how to use email effectively. If you want additional information, the following sites provide useful information:

- *Emoticons:* www.pb.org/emoticon.html and www.demon.net
- *Acronyms:* www.acronyms.ch and www.acronymfinder.com
- *Email:* www.everythingemail.net and http://email.about.com

1. When to use email

Before you send email, consider your audience and the situation. Then, decide whether email is the right medium for your message.

Use email when:

You need to communicate efficiently:

- *Contact someone* who is not available
- *Send the same message* to several people instantaneously
- *Deliver your message* inexpensively
- *Send a forwardable message*
- *Transfer* sounds, video clips, programs, and pictures

You need to communicate written information:

- *Detailed:* Convey detailed information, such as specific budget amounts, names, or phone numbers
- *Not private:* Send a message that is not private or confidential
- *Fast:* Get a quick, written response
- *Record:* Have a record of the communication
- *Easy to distribute:* Distribute documents, especially when receivers will need a soft copy to edit

Do not use email when:

- The information you need to convey is *sensitive* (email is not private)
- The message should be *delivered personally* (e.g., bad news needs face to face)
- You are concerned about *how your message looks and is formatted*
- You need to get *immediate feedback* from several people or to build consensus in a group

2. How to use effective reader access techniques

When email is the right medium for your message, use the following tips to ensure your reader can access the information easily.

Write informative subject lines   Many busy professionals decide whether to read or delete messages based on the sender and subject line. What you write in the subject line can determine whether your message gets read. Do not just reply to a previous message or joke and leave the same subject line.

Write accurate subject lines that tell the reader what, when, where, and other important information. Put the critical information toward the beginning of the subject line because some programs display only the first few words in the summary/inbox screen. Other advantages of informative subject lines are that recipients may not have to open the message again to obtain critical information, and may know how time critical the information is.

> *Example of a poorly written subject line*
>   RE: The Bell Project

> *Example of a more effective subject line*
>   Urgent meeting May 2 re Bell Project

Present your key ideas quickly   Studies show that most employees do not read past the first screen of an email message. If you can, limit your message to one screen. But even if your message is more than one page, your first screen should present all of the main ideas, including your agenda or preview. Leave background and supplemental information for the end of the message.

Example: Main ideas first, easy access, and short paragraphs

Use easy-access techniques in the body of your message. Use displayed lists with bullets or hyphens rather than paragraph lists when appropriate. Use short sentences, short paragraphs, and ample headings.

Use shorter paragraphs and shorter sentences than in other printed documents. Remember the limited screen size and design your message for easy reader access.

The example on the next page shows an email message with the main ideas first, easy access, and short paragraphs.

3. How to write audience-focused messages

Use a conversational, professional tone when you write   The spontaneous nature of email tends to invite a casual writing style. However, be cautious of sounding too casual in business messages. Use a businesslike approach in your emails at work and make sure your messages are well organized.

Be aware of how different people use email   In some companies, email is used for urgent, time-critical messages. In other companies, email is not used much for anything. Remember that not everyone with email addresses checks their email regularly. In some companies, proofreading is essential; in other companies, all lowercase and poor spelling is the time-saving norm.

Avoid using all capital letters   Using all capitals is associated with *flaming,* shouting or yelling. Also, using all capitals makes the writing harder to read.

> *For example:*
>> THIS IS CONSIDERED ANGRY SHOUTING!
>> This is considered polite conversation.

Do not assume that everyone appreciates emoticons and abbreviations.   Some see *emoticons* as silly and unprofessional. Many will feel frustrated if you use abbreviations they are not familiar with. If you choose to lighten your message using emoticons, here are a few commonly used ones.

4. How to send email

Review your messages carefully before sending them   In many companies, email is used for rapid communication. However, even if you are close friends with the colleague to whom you are sending the message, you may not be sure to whom your colleague will forward the message. Studies show that people make judgments about your intelligence, education, professionalism, and social status based on your grammar and spelling.

EXAMPLES OF EMOTICONS
:)   A friendly smile—expresses happiness or pleasure.
: (A frown—shows frustration, anger, sadness, or empathy.
;)   A wink—expresses joking, kidding, or signals an inside joke.
: - o   A surprised look—expresses surprise or shock.

Example: Alphabetized Recipient addresses, a blind carbon copy,
a professional signature, and a file attached

Screen shot reprinted by permission from Microsoft Corporation.

Do not send email messages when you are angry　　Sometimes, your opinions change after you've had a chance to think about the issue more. Sometimes, you get more information that helps you see the matter in a different light. Give yourself time to cool off before sending your message.

Remember that email is not private　　Your employer can read both your incoming and outgoing mail. Just because you have a password does not mean your messages are private.

Beware of missent and unreceived messages

- *Send to correct audience.* If your message is intended for one individual, be careful to send it only to that person. Some get in trouble by using the incorrect reply button, and accidentally sending a personal message to the entire group of recipients of the initial message.
- *Check attachments.* **Attachments** and other formatted messages often do not translate from one server to another server with different software. Be sure to attach the files you intend to include with your email.

Do not send unnecessary email Do not spend work time and the company's computer resources sending and receiving unnecessary email. Do not use email to gossip or criticize. Do not forward chain letters. Further, some "jokes" and silly messages, even if deleted, can be accessed and used as evidence in age, race, religious, and gender discrimination lawsuits.

Know and follow your company's email policy Many businesses ask employees not to use the company's email system for personal messages. Even if there is not a written policy, it may be a good idea to access your personal email before or after work from a personal account at home. Do not consider any of your email at work to be private.

Alphabetize recipients' addresses Alphabetizing the list will help you avoid sending signals about hierarchy and importance of recipients. Also, it will be easier for recipients to skim the list and to check to see if you sent the message to a certain person. (Of course, if you want to send signals about hierarchy, put names in order of importance.)

Use special features to hide other readers Use blind carbon copy (BCC) or recipient list suppressed if you don't want the recipients to have the names or addresses of the others who receive the message. For example, suppress the list if you are sending a response to all who applied to a job or if you want to protect a large number of recipients from *spam.*

Use an automatic professional signature at the end of your emails Include your full name, title, address, phone and fax numbers, and web address. This will aid recipients if they need to call you or to send you something via *snail mail.*

The example on the facing page shows an email message in Microsoft Outlook with alphabetized recipient addresses (see *To:* box), a blind carbon copy (see *Bcc* box), a professional signature (see bottom of message text), and a file attached (see *potscommissions* after message text).

5. How to manage the email you receive

Read your professional email frequently Even if your company does not rely heavily on email, often you will interact with colleagues from other organizations who expect you to read and respond to their emails promptly.

Respond to emails promptly   Often, email messages are short and do not require a lengthy answer. If you can, respond to the message as soon as you read it. This shows your responsiveness and saves you the time it takes to reaccess and reread the message you received. Consider sending a short, polite response to emails that don't demand an answer, such as, "Thanks for the info. Hope you have fun on your trip." Delete unimportant emails after you have responded to them.

Print hard copies of messages you need to save in files   Print and file messages, such as messages that should go in employees' personnel files and messages that provide legal documentation.

Use an effective storage technique for messages you need to save   Most businesses limit the amount of email an employee can store on the server. Many programs automatically delete the oldest messages to limit the mailbox size. Thus, you should save messages and addresses you need to keep on your hard disk or on a floppy disk. Organize your messages into files in a way that makes sense to you, such as by sender, project, or type (policy messages, employee requests, etc.).

Use an automatic email reply when you will not be checking your messages   For example, if you go out of the country and do not plan to check your email, set up an automatic reply to be sent in response to all incoming emails. Provide contact information for matters that can't wait until your return.

III. FAXES

Faxes are useful and efficient because they transmit paper copy immediately and because they can communicate information that involves more than just text—for example, letters, business forms, graphs, drawings, charts, photos, newspaper clippings, and drafts with markings. The following guidelines will help you send your fax efficiently.

1. When to fax

To decide whether faxing is the best medium to use, analyze your audience and what kind of document you need to send. Also, consider the advantages and disadvantages of fax machines such as time and cost or privacy considerations. Here are some guidelines when deciding what to do.

Use faxes when you have:

- *Time-sensitive documents,* since fax machines can deliver documents within a matter of minutes
- *Hard copy of graphics*
- *Drafts with markings* the reader needs to see
- *Documents requiring signatures* of people not present

Do not use faxes when:

- *Privacy is an issue.* Generally fax machines are located in an area where many eyes will see the fax.
- *You have doubt about routing.* If you have not faxed the reader before, find out about routing. Offices may or may not have a sorting or routing system. Be sure the receiver knows about the transmission.
- *Sending unsolicited advertisements.*

2. How to fax

After deciding that faxing is the best method for achieving your over-all goal, make sure the document is formatted properly and will result in a successful transmission.

Effective documents

- *Include a cover page* that states recipient's name, sender's name and number, date, number of pages, and a brief message describing purpose of the fax.

- *Use a readable font,* between 12 and 18 points. Some fax machines blur the text, so larger is better.

- *Use ample margins* of 1 to 1.5 inches on all four sides. Fax machines tend to reduce and cut off edges, so take this into account.

- *Do not send documents that will not fax well.* Do not use wrinkled, creased, curled, torn, carbon-coated/-backed paper, or onion or thin paper. Remove all clips and staples. Allow correction fluid to dry.

Effective transmission

- *Make sure the recipient has the necessary resources for receiving a fax.* Is the company organized to receive, sort, and deliver the fax? What are the company's policies regarding fax machines?

- *If the document is time sensitive, notify the recipient the fax is coming.* Also confirm the recipient received the fax. Otherwise, time-sensitive documents may not be received in time.

TYPES OF ELECTRONIC DISCUSSION FORUMS				
Factor	**Bulletin Usenet**	**Email Boards**	**Real-Time Groups**	**Chat**
Real time				x
Public	x	x	x	x
Private		x	x	x
Moderated	x	x	x	x
Unmoderated	x	x	x	x
Board posted	x	x		x
Email delivered			x	

IV. ELECTRONIC DISCUSSION FORUMS

Electronic **discussion forums** can be a valuable professional resource. Online chats can be an excellent source of specialized information. You can often ask qualified experts specific questions and get quick, insightful responses. You can stay involved in up-to-date conversations in your field of expertise. Also, employers frequently announce job openings on newsgroups related to the company's area of expertise.

Electronic discussion groups can be either sequential or *real-time* interactive: (1) sequential groups post messages that either remain in an online forum to be read, or are sent to participants' email addresses, thus, can be read when the participants have time to be involved; (2) real-time groups are online at the same time and communicate almost instantaneously.

The following sections define and describe various discussion media, including sequential discussion forums (the Usenet, bulletin board [*BBS*] groups, email discussion groups) and real-time discussion forums (real-time chat groups). The chart above lists the characteristics of the electronic discussion forums discussed in this chapter.

The end of this section offers tips for communicating in electronic groups.

1. How to access sequential discussion forums

Sequential discussion forums   Three common types of sequential discussion are the Usenet, electronic bulletin boards, and email groups. Each will be discussed in turn.

The Usenet   The WWW *Usenet* is a repository of thousands of discussion groups. It contains over 20,000 different publicly available groups. It has been around longer than most of the other discussion forums. Participants post messages on bulletin boards in groups that generally are not moderated. Advice about newsgroup etiquette and tips on how to post messages is available in the group news. announce.newusers.

To access the Usenet, you can:

- *Visit special Internet sites* such as www.remarq.com or www.deja.com because they provide the additional advantage that you can search for specific subject matter, not just broad topics and newsgroup names.

- *See postings of general newsgroups* at www.cuc.edu/cgi-bin/listserv-form.pl and see lists of business newsgroups at http://sunsite.org.uk/ public/usenet/news-faqs/

- *Use software programs* such as Free Agent or NewsWatcher.

Other bulletin board groups   In addition to the Usenet, thousands of other electronic discussion groups are available. Whereas the Usenet is often unmoderated, public, and anyone can contribute, other discussion forums are sometimes private and often moderated. You must join the group to *post* messages. Many professional organizations and web sites host their own private and by-invitation-only discussion groups.

- *To join:* Most major **ISPs (Internet service providers)** offer hundreds of groups. The following free URLs provide discussion groups:
  www.netzero.com
  www.yahoo.com
  www.juno.com
  www.NBCi.com

  The following URLs list financial and stock discussion groups:
  www.ragingbull.com

www.siliconeinvestor.com
www.motleyfool.com

- *To set up:* The following sites help you set up discussion forums.

  www.groupvine.com: Allows you to make members-only discussion groups. Team members can post written comments, pictures, and audio files.

  www.intranets.com: Provides an easy way for organizations to set up a central place for team members to post and access information.

Email discussion groups   Whereas electronic bulletin board participants must go to a special group site to send and receive messages, participants in email groups receive messages in their email boxes without having to go to a special group site. Sometimes, these email groups are sponsored by a company or professional organization, and sometimes these groups are organized on an ad-hoc basis by private individuals. Some are private; some are available to anyone. A popular site for setting up free public and private email discussion groups is www.egroups.com.

2. How to access real-time discussion forums

In real-time discussion forums, participants are online at the same time. Many ISPs offer a variety of real-time discussion forums.

Advantages and disadvantages   The advantage is that real-time discussions can feel more personal, since participants know that others are online at the same time. However, sometimes these discussions are shallow because participants usually don't take the time to compose long, thoughtful responses.

Business uses   Many organizations are using online chat as a way to stay in touch with employees, customers, and colleagues. Some of these systems allow users to see which people from their contact list are currently online and available to instantly receive a message. This can be an effective communication channel for some immediate business messages.

Resources   Several companies offer various levels of interactive discussion software that allows you to set up a real-time forum:

- *www.mirabillis.com:* Offers a free online chat software program called ICQ (I seek you) and sells upgraded chat software as well.

COMMON NETICISMS USED ONLINE	
BTW	By the way
FWIW	For what it's worth
IMHO	In my humble opinion
OTOH	On the other hand
ROTFL	Rolling on the floor laughing
RTFM	Read the ____ manual
TTFN	Ta ta for now

- *www.ichat.com:* Offers free browser-integrated software that allows users to chat one on one or to host large-scale events online; sells upgraded software as well.
- *www.eshare.com:* eShare Technologies Inc. sells its Expressions Interaction Suite for around $4,000 for 50 users.

3. How to participate in electronic discussion forums

Once you have accessed an electronic discussion forum, you need to know how to be a successful group member.

Effective participation   The following tips will help you be an effective participant:

- *Spend some time reading* the newsgroup's messages before posting your own comment or question.
- *Do not believe everything that is written.* People are not always who they say they are. Participants sometimes have hidden agendas that motivate them to lie.
- *Before posting a question,* make sure the question has not already been answered. Most groups have *FAQ (frequently asked questions)* lists.
- *When using online chats in an organization,* distribute biographies and other information before the meeting so participants can get to know each other.
- *Consider limiting the number of participants* who are allowed to type comments; this can help keep the conversation focused. Groups of five or fewer work best.

- *Use the **chat room** to identify interesting people,* then move to email conversations or one-on-one chat rooms to communicate with them.

Effective posting techniques   The following suggestions will help you to post effective messages:

- *Subject line:* Compose a clear, specific, informative subject line.
- *Messages:* Write audience-focused, short, concise, well-organized messages.
- *Typography:* Don't use ALL CAPITAL letters, since this is considered rude.
- *Polite messages:* Don't send rude or impolite messages or make personal attacks (a.k.a. ***flaming***).
- *References:* When responding to a previous message, refer to that message specifically.
- *Proofread:* Review your messages before sending them; you can lose credibility and look stupid when you make spelling and grammatical mistakes; check for appropriate tone as well.
- *Avoid:* Don't use abbreviations or ***neticisms*** that haven't already been used in the group. Here are some common neticisms you may see used online.

V. MULTIMEDIA BUSINESS CARDS

Ordinary business cards have been used for decades. However, they are limited as to the amount and type of information they can contain. Multimedia business cards combine the convenience of a business card with the multimedia power and interactivity of a CD-ROM. These CD cards are also called e-cards, electronic business cards, and CD business cards. The following picture is an actual size image of an e-card used by Lakeside Software.

What they are   Multimedia business cards are usually the same size as ordinary business cards, but can hold between 35 *MB* (megabytes) and 100 MB of information. They also come in different shapes, such as square, gear-shaped, and octagonal. Business card–sized e-cards hold 35 MB of information, whereas larger cards can hold over 100 MB of information. Multimedia business cards can contain video clips, web links, music clips, pictures, and anything else than can be put on a regular CD. They are used for training, advertising, software distribution, and other times when you want to provide a large amount of information in a small package.

Source: Lakeside Software, Inc.

Multimedia business cards can be used in a variety of ways. An applicant or sales associate can put her entire resume, portfolio, full-color catalog, or interactive teaching program on the card. A travel agent can put video clips of exotic vacation destinations as well as pricing information on the CD. A real estate agent can provide a virtual walk-through of an exclusive property he has for sale, with a picture of the home printed on the outside of the card. E-cards can be made to look like standard business cards with name, address, phone number, and company logo printed on the outside.

Advantages and disadvantages

- *Advantages:* (1) Compact size makes it easy for the recipient to carry; (2) interesting media make them more memorable than traditional business cards; (3) content can be interactive.

- *Disadvantages:* (1) Expensive to produce, they often cost over $2 each (thus, they are more expensive to give away than a paper business card); (2) hard to update; (3) require the reader to use a computer to view contents.

How to get more information   The following sites offer additional information about multimedia business cards:

> www.bizcardsoncd.com
> www.digital-card.com
> www.flatspinmedia.com
> www.moving-eye.co.uk
> www.multi-medialive.net/mmlive
> www.1jn.com/mbizcard.html

Because of the increasing amount of new technology that depends on written communication, your skills in using these communication media are more important than ever. By following the suggestions in this chapter, you will be a more efficient and more effective communicator at work.

CHAPTER 4 OUTLINE

I. SET YOUR WEB SITE STRATEGY
   1. Analyze your purpose
   2. Analyze your audience

II. PLAN AND DESIGN THE SITE
   1. Perform preliminary research
   2. Map out the site
   3. Write your content
   4. Design the site to work as a whole
   5. Choosing your graphics
   6. Use helpful web sites
   7. Fine-tune the site design

III. MANAGE YOUR WEB SITE
   1. Finding a name and a host
   2. Attract visitors to your site

CHAPTER 4

Designing Web Pages

A s the Internet has grown over the years, the number of web sites has increased dramatically, creating a highly competitive market for Internet users' time as well as dollars. According to a survey by the Internet Software Consortium, the number of new domains has grown from just a few to over a million in one decade.

When you think about the Internet market, think in terms of what a *market* used to mean. Buyers and sellers interacted as sales took place; buyers talked with other buyers about the products and with sellers about their satisfaction or desires. Regardless of whether you use the web to buy or sell, this analogy shows that a web site is about ongoing communication, about having conversations.

This chapter provides a basic introduction to one of the fastest-growing areas of electronic communication—web design. You will learn how to (1) set your strategy, (2) plan and design the site, and (3) manage your site.

Increase in the Number of Internet Domains

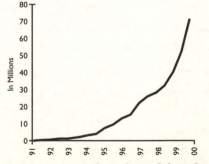

Source: Internet Software Consortium (www.isc.org)

I. SET YOUR WEB SITE STRATEGY

Just as in all communication situations, you start your web page design by analyzing your purpose, objectives, and audience. By defining your objectives before you begin, you will be more efficient, because you won't waste time designing material that is not consistent with your purpose. Also, you will be more effective, because your site will be specifically tailored to be clear and persuasive for your target audience.

1. Analyze your purpose

When designing a web site, you must first define your overall purpose. You may want to entertain, provide information, develop goodwill, promote and produce sales, or secure donations.

Set specific objectives   Once you have identified the reason for having a web site, decide what you want the web site to accomplish. You must be specific about these objectives. For example, if you work for a nonprofit organization, your overall purpose may be to gain donations, but to get those donations, you want visitors to the site to:

- Learn how your organization contributes to society
- Believe the organization makes an important contribution
- Be convinced the organization is well run and professional
- Understand the ways they can contribute to the organization
- Conclude that even small contributions are worth making
- Become personally involved with your project

  In addition, you want visitors to:

- Find it easy to make donations
- Make donations online
- Make repeat donations
- Encourage others to make donations

Analyze relationships among objectives   Figure out the relationships among the objectives. You may want to prioritize objectives, establish a linear list, or chart out the ways they relate to each other. For example, until visitors to your site know what you do, they can't believe you make an important contribution, and unless they perceive the organization as well run and professional, they aren't going to make contributions to your particular organization, even if you've convinced them your aims are laudable. If visitors don't understand how to make contributions and you don't make contributing easy or within their budgets, they will leave your site without donating and take their money elsewhere. In addition, you need readers to become personally involved with the project so they are more likely to make repeat donations and to encourage others to donate to the organization.

2. Analyze your audience

As with all other areas in web design, your audience analysis needs to be detailed and complete. Look not just at your audience in general, but ask yourself what variety of people will visit the site and whether they have differing interests, needs, or motives. Ask yourself questions such as "What is their educational background?" and "How important are graphics to them?" For example, if you sell used books, you may have visitors with at least a high school education who want to find a specific book quickly, order it online, and be willing to pay extra to have it shipped immediately. Other visitors will be browsing and thus be more interested in your site's having a variety of indexes so they can browse by author, subject, and title, and read reviews of new books. Some visitors will want you to look for a specific book or edition for them and may be willing to wait months for that particular book. You will want to set up your site to accommodate all the visitors, or, perhaps, if some visitors will want services you don't provide, your site can contain links to other sites that do offer those services.

Start analyzing your audience by thinking about who will visit your site and what kind of conversation you could have with them. For example, if your site provides company information, what do you know about your employees that may affect their behavior? Are they mostly driven, busy, and experienced computer operators? If so, speed is a factor, but you can assume familiarity with computers and web *navigation*. They may want a way to provide feedback about company policy, goals, or benefits.

If you're a nonprofit organization that helps protect ecologically vital lands and animals, your visitors may be mostly middle to upper class, have a college education, like to garden, view the world in broad and long-term perspectives, and make donations to other nonprofits.

If you're selling a product, think about who buys that kind of product. You can find out information about customers on the web from surveys, articles, or competing or similar companies. Business sites may offer the most help.

Your audience analysis will affect all the rest of your decisions as you complete the design for your web page, and you should also use it to review your decisions about content to make sure you have factored in your audience.

II. PLAN AND DESIGN THE SITE

Once you know your purpose, it's time to start planning the design
of your site. This section describes how to conduct research to determine how your site should be designed, to map out the site, to write
the content, to design the site to work as a whole, to choose effective graphics, to use helpful web sites, and to fine-tune the site
design.

1. Perform preliminary research.

Design the site as a whole, not just individual pages. As you design,
keep in mind your objectives and audience analysis and your need to
provide form that functions well.

- *Research on Internet behavior:* Keep in mind what researchers have
  learned about people's behavior on the Internet. A few general facts
  are that anywhere from 10 to 40 percent of your visitors will not go
  beyond the ***home page*** of your site (depending on whose research you
  believe) and that readers want skimmable text, easy navigation, and an
  easy way to purchase or respond to the information you've provided.
  Remember the idea of the marketplace? Visitors today want to be able
  to get help, to find more information, and to tell you about their experience with your site or your products—they want to have conversations.

- *Research on your purpose:* In addition to using general information
  about how people search and use the web, you can do research that is
  specific to your purpose or product. In fact, unless you are strictly an
  e-commerce company, your company already has information that can
  help you gear your site to the needs and behaviors of prospective customers or visitors. You can also visit similar sites. Look at what they
  have done well, what you can improve on, and what information is
  useful to you. Then, look for ways you can innovate or give your site
  a unique twist.

- *Research popular sites:* Analyze the design of popular sites. Go to
  www.worldbestwebsites.com This site analyzes web design, gives
  awards to the best sites, and contains links to the award-winning sites.
  The top five retail sites, according to *PC Data/InfoWorld,* are listed in
  the table on the following page.

TOP FIVE RETAIL SITES		
Site	Unique Users (in millions)	August 2000 Buyers
amazon.com	19.0	1,607,000
ticketmaster.com	5.4	595,000
buy.com	3.6	466,000
cdnow.com	7.3	441,000
sears.com	4.1	359,000

Source: PC Data/InfoWorld, September 25, 2000.

Web design is not a linear task. It involves keeping a whole range of factors in mind and checking to be sure your design includes each factor. Thus far, we've discussed analyzing your purpose and audience and performing preliminary research. The next sections will describe how to map out your site, write your content, design the site, choose the graphics, use helpful web sites, fine-tune the site, and manage the site.

2. Map out the site

Your next step is mapping out the site. Some designers recommend working first with pencil and paper: even if you can't draw well, you can sketch out the overall site and label visuals. Working with pencil and paper will allow you to spread out the pages and look at the whole site at once, arranging and rearranging, and drawing in relationships to help you decide how the pages will be linked. Once you have the first draft of your pages, you can transfer the design to a wall-sized sheet of paper, a large white board, or a storyboard that visually shows the relationship between the pages.

3. Write your content

A web site is only as good as its written text. Even more than other written documents, it must be concise, easy to read, and interesting. In addition, research has shown that readers want skimmable text. Choose your style and language based on your purpose and audience analysis. Do you want your web site to convey a professional image, to be fun and inviting, to get visitors personally involved, to highlight the unique points of your product and differentiate it from the competition? Each different purpose and prospective audience will affect how you write. For more information on audiences and persuasion, see Chapter 1 in the *Guide to Managerial Communication.*

Some of your objectives will determine content while others may determine other functions you may need. Using the earlier example, you may decide you need an email newsletter to keep donators up to date and encouraged to return, or individual emails to say thanks for a donation. That email could tell donators specific information about how their donations were used so they can envision their money in action and feel personally involved. You can also include a way for visitors to send the URL to friends they think may be interested in your organization.

The next step is to identify the specific content your site will include. An outline you tie to your objectives is helpful. If you also have an offline entity, make sure your content is consistent with that entity. Once you've identified content based on your objectives, it's time to analyze your audience. Again, this step must be specific. Regardless of the audience, all web pages should use:

- Short paragraphs
- Many headings
- Interesting graphics to supplement the text
- Enhanced type (bold, italics, etc.)

Web pages today are often created by a team of professionals. Don't overlook the need for professional editors and writers. The written text is so important that it's worth spending some money to ensure that your site is easy to read and professional.

4. Design the site to work as a whole

Home page considerations Given that you should design the whole site and not individual pages, the home page still has some unique considerations. To get viewers into your site, your first page must:

- *Come up quickly* (at least some images or text must be readable within four to eight seconds)
- *Be easily identifiable*
- *Have an easy-to-use directory* of main topics and subtopics
- *Grab viewers' attention,* and entice them to delve further into the site
- *Mirror brand-building efforts* in other places, if relevant to your company

Although some designers work straight from HTML, many designers recommend working with a ***WYSIWYG (What You See Is What You Get)*** page builder so you can work with layout and content and not wade through hypertext language. However you choose to approach the design, keep the overall site in mind as well as specific needs such as navigation and graphics.

Effortless navigation   The easier it is to navigate your site, the greater the number of people who will explore beyond the first page and the greater your chances will be of reaching your objectives. Here are some ways to make navigation easy:

- *Organize content for easy comprehension* by including a list of topics and subtopics on the home page so all visitors have to do is point and click to find the specific information they want. Visitors should be able to skim the home page and understand how the site works. Avoid unnecessary words and pictures that distract visitors from your main content.

- *Provide access.* Give the variety of users for whom you've designed your site ways to use the site for what they want. For instance, if different users want to search the site using different categories, provide clear directions that explain the categories.

- *Make movement from one page to another simple.* Don't make visitors scroll through page by page, but give them a way of easily jumping from one page to another. Organize pages by subject and design buttons to take visitors directly to each area. These buttons should remain at the top, bottom, or side of the screen the whole time the visitor is at your site.

- *Keep navigation consistent* throughout the site and position the navigational aids logically.

- *Provide only important, high-quality, external links,* and make sure readers can tell what they will find at the linked site.

- *Use writing techniques to provide reader access,* such as several levels of headings, lists, and text boxes. Avoid large blocks of text, such as long paragraphs. Instead, use visual cues to show your readers how the site is organized. For example, you may want to display a second-level outline that shows major sections as well as lists of topics or categories within those sections. (For a more detailed discussion on ways to increase reader access, see *Guide to Managerial Communication,* Chapter III.)

- *Make sure each page clearly identifies the site* and indicates where it fits in the site. Many visitors to your web site will not see the home page. Some visitors will type in a detailed URL that takes them to a specific page, and others will enter via a link from another web site that you may or may not be aware of.

- *Check out the latest ways to ensure that navigation is graceful and simple* on your site before completing your design. Since computer technology is changing rapidly, one source for up-to-date information is web sites. Pages 62–63 list web design sites that contain this information.

5. Choose your graphics

When choosing graphics for your web site, remember the great design adage: "Less is more." Sharp, professional graphics keep a site from being boring, highlight content, simplify navigation, and make your site unique. However, it's all too easy to distract viewers from the very content you want them to understand by using visuals that are too dominant, flashy, or that do not match the style of your web site.

Design for a professional look   You don't want your site to look like a mix of individual styles and tastes. You want your web page to look like a unified whole designed by a team. Make sure all pages in the site are consistent in terms of:

- *Colors:* Choose colors that look good together and evoke the feeling you want to convey.

- *Typography:* Use font styles that are consistent with the personality of your organization. Use font colors and sizes strategically.

- *Layout:* Apply the same general style of layout for all pages in your site. Use a layout that is both logical and eye pleasing.

- *Balance:* Make sure each page is balanced in terms of white space, graphics, use of color, and so on.

- *Graphics:* Use graphic styles that work well together. Don't have one style of drawings on one page in your site and another style of drawings on another page.

The following list contains a few of the choices you can make to give your graphics a professional look:

- *Use actual photographs rather than* **clip art.** Although some clip art may work well, photos generally look more professional. Photoshop will allow you to make dropouts, crop small sections, manipulate color and contrast, or produce a host of other variations from any photograph.
- *Avoid shapes that have visual connotations* of being closed or static, such as squares. You can either create less regular shapes or make the shapes appear to be less regular.
- *Use attractive colors.* Check how the colors appear on a variety of browsers. Use the advice offered for slides in Chapter 5 of this book: Choose contrasting colors for the background and the text.
- *Balance variety with repetition.* Use enough variety to avoid boredom, but use repetition to give unity.

Choose visuals that load quickly   In addition to needing graphics that look professional, you need graphics that load quickly. You can optimize speed by using simple visuals, sketches that are completed further in the site, ***thumbnails*** that can be enlarged if the visitor chooses, vector-based graphics such as Flash, software that compresses images such as DjVu, or streaming media. Before you decide on graphics, you may want to explore the most recently developed options for optimizing loading speed and quality. When considering speed, compare the different file types you can use for your graphics. The most common graphics file types are shown in the table on page 61 and are described in the following paragraphs.

- ***Bitmap files,*** *with the extension ".bmp",* store all of the information describing every pixel on the screen. Thus, they are clear but require a great deal of memory and download slowly.
- ***JPEG files,*** *with extension ".jpg",* can contain over 16 million colors, are also good for photographs. However, once you convert a file to JPEG format, you lose some color information that you cannot get back unless you've saved a copy in another format (e.g., .bmp or .tif).

Because you lose color information when you convert a file into a JPEG, they are called *lossy*.

* **GIF files,** *with the extension ".gif",* contain only 256 colors. These files load quickly and work well for simple illustrations and graphics. Also, you can convert a file from a slower-loading bitmap into a faster-loading GIF and back into a bitmap without losing any quality. Because you don't lose any quality when converting your files into GIFs, GIFs are described as *lossless*.

One caution: The newest technology has a strong lure, but evaluate what it can do to further your purpose before acquiring the program. Some technology may be particularly applicable to your web site. For example, DjVu allows scanned images to be condensed to compression values as high as 1000:1. Those images will load quickly, but can be examined section by section because even blown up very large, they don't pixelate but retain their high quality. If you provide an online catalog for an auction house, **DjVu technology** will provide

COMMON TYPES OF GRAPHIC FILES				
File Type	**Size**	**Description**	**Advantages**	**Disadvantages**
.bmp	457K	Uncompressed bitmap file; can contain over 16 million colors	High-quality image; contains all color information	Loads slowly; takes more room to store
.jpg	142K	Compressed 24-bit bitmap file; can contain over 16 million colors	Loads more quickly and takes less disk storage space than .bmp files	Does not save all of the original color information (lossy)
.gif	121K	Compressed 16-bit bitmap file; contains only 256 colors; lossless	Loads quickly; saves all the original color information; uses less disk storage space	Colors may not look as natural or vibrant

a strong benefit. But if you don't need its attributes, any technology is too expensive.

When you're searching for appropriate graphics, look at what other web sites have used and check out the free graphics and design help offered, as explained in the next section.

6. Use helpful web sites

The web itself can be a source for help in designing web sites. However, as in all other areas, the quality of the sites differs radically. Many sites contain good ideas but don't provide enough information to be very helpful. Other sites offer tutorials that aren't well designed or complete. And some tutorials use hard-and-fast rules or structures that do not match your needs or your users' needs. In addition, the web is changing so rapidly that what's new today won't be by next month.

Sites offering general web design advice   Visit sites that offer a variety of web-related services and information because they are updated frequently, and they have articles and reviews of the best books and software, a wide variety of information including tutorials, and numerous links to helpful sites. If you can't find the information you want on one of these sites, you should be able to find information about other places you can get current and high-quality help. Try the following sites:

- *www.informationweek.com:* Contains product reviews, a TechEncyclopedia, news, web tools, reader services, advertiser services, and many links to TechWeb sites.

- *www.webdeveloper.com:* Contains the Webpedia, an online dictionary and search engine for computer and Internet technology, forur .s, reviews, tool news, and a large and detailed pull-down directory of specific topics. Don't let the somewhat confusing home page deter you from exploring this site.

- *www.windweaver.com/searchpage7.htm:* Gives web design and style resources, articles, forums, magazines, guides, graphics, search pages, and links to many other helpful sites.

- *http://members.tripod.com/~WebGenies/:* Offers a complete web design clinic, as well as information about HTML and coding, graphics, and web content.

- *www.webreview.com:* Includes a search function, sections for guides, reviews, articles, tools, resources, authoring, design, development, e-commerce, and multimedia.

Sites offering specific information

- *www.benedict.com:* Offers a great deal of helpful information about copyrights; provides discourse and invites solutions for copyright difficulties on the Internet.

- *www.graphic-design.com/Web/Default.html:* Provides hundreds of graphics that are available to download.

- *www.nua-tech.com/paddy/promote.shtml#intr:* Takes you through the design process from designing to submitting the site in an article written for Nua-Tech.

Sites with style and writing guides

- *www.cal.bemidji.msus.edu/WebTraining/Resources.html:* Offers carefully filtered lists and links for web style manuals, web design, writing for the web, web page review, and critique from Bemidji State University in Minnesota.

- *www.owl.english.purdue.edu:* Gives advice on writing effective documents, links to other helpful sites, and assistance with grammar from Purdue University.

- *www.info.med.yale.edu/caim/manual/contents.html:* Provides a web design style manual for high-quality design and writing from Yale University.

Other helpful sites

- *Graphics:* You can find "15 Favorite Graphic Design Resources" at www.lightlink.com/xine/graphics.html. In addition to graphics resources that range from free high-quality art images to a color selection guide and a wide variety of fonts, this site has links to sound sources, a place to submit your site to multiple search engines, and advice on site promotion.

- *Professional designers:* If you decide to hire professional designers to help you with your site, www.webdesignlist.com provides a national list of hundreds of web design firms.

- *Magazines:* Another source for current web design information is magazines.

www.internetworld.com: Contains a calendar of events, data about new site features that designers include, and free product information.

www.infoworld.com: Offers a vast amount of computer-related information including information technology (IT) news, networking advice, test center analyses of software programs, and a gripe line.

7. Fine-tune the site design

After the site is designed, you need to examine the site in a variety of ways from a variety of perspectives. Look at the site as a whole. Use a visitor's perspective and the following checklists.

Is the site suited to your purpose and audience?

- *Check to see that the site will fulfill your purpose,* checking each individual objective you identified.

- *Have several different people edit and proofread the site:* The grammar and spelling should be immaculate.

- *Ask for feedback from outside sources.* Invite a variety of people who were not involved with the design to try out the site.

- *Have visitors identify any instructions that lack clarity* and evaluate the use of the site, including their gut reaction to it. You want visitors to like being on your web site.

Is the site easy to use and efficient?

- *Does the site load quickly and efficiently?* Note that when the site is on your local machine for development it will run much faster than when it is on the web. Also, test your site from a modem. Don't let your company's high-speed phone lines give you a false sense of speed.

- *Can a visitor tell what's on the site and how to get to different areas easily?* Ask people from outside your company to use the site while you watch.

- *Is navigation through the site smooth and simple?* Watch how the people from outside your company move from page to page. Are they overlooking the easiest ways to get around?

Is the content in the site appropriate?

- *Does the site cater to the interests* and needs of the variety of visitors you identified?

- *Is the home page attractive and inviting?*
- *Does the site create a unified whole?*
- *Have you provided visitors a way to converse with employees (if applicable)?*

Once you have chosen the details such as specific colors, graphics, fonts, and images, check the overall design of your site again. Make sure your visuals, everything from colors and fonts to images, maintain the style you have chosen, provide continuity, and support your purpose. Images should emphasize, explain, or provide visual definition.

III. MANAGE YOUR WEB SITE

Once you have your site designed, it's time to get it up and running. This section will describe how to choose and register your domain name, find a *host,* attract visitors, and keep it updated.

1. Find a name and a host

A World Wide Web site name, or URL, has three components. First, it starts with www. Second, it has a unique name for your site. Third, it ends with a suffix, such as .com (a commercial site), .edu (an education site), .org (an organization), or .gov (a government site).

Finding a name   Your most challenging aspect of registering a domain name is finding a unique, easy-to-remember name for your site. If you're making a site for an existing company, a good choice is your company's name, with no spaces between the words. A second choice is to put hyphens between the words. Often, you need to get quite creative to find a name that hasn't been taken already.

To find out which site names have been taken already, go to a web site that helps people register domain names. To find one, ask your browser to search for "domain name." Three popular domain name sales sites are www.internic.com, www.register.com, and www.tabnet.com. These sites have all the information you need for finding a unique name and registering and paying for your domain name.

Registering and paying   It costs about $50 a year to keep a domain name. Remember to keep paying your bill for your domain name. If you don't pay, you will lose your domain name. Even Microsoft had its Hot Mail service go down for forgetting to pay the small domain registration fee.

Finding a host   After you have designed your site and registered a domain name, you must post the site on a computer. If you're already using a major ISP for your Internet connection, and pleased with the service you've received, you may want to ask that company if they host web pages. You can compare their services and prices to others. Many hosting companies have web sites. Also, some sites list hundreds of hosting services, enabling you to easily find the ones that match your criteria. See, for example, www.tophosts.com. In addition, some companies will host small web sites for free (e.g., www.NBCi.com, www.tripod.lycos.com, and www.geocities.com). These hosting sites get paid by flashing ads to all of the visitors to your site.

2. Attract visitors to your site

Before you can advertise your site, you must complete some behind-the-scenes work such as choosing *keywords* and creating *metatags*. Then, you can submit your site to search engines and use other methods of advertising.

Determine keywords   To get visitors to your site, you will need to determine what category terms and keywords will help searchers find your site. One way to choose keywords is to ask Internet-experienced customers or members of your intended audience what keywords they would use to search for your site. Then, check competitors' sites, especially those that show up near the top of search results and look both for terms that will pick out your site and terms you want to avoid because they associate you with undesirable sites.

Once you have a list of keywords, try several searches using different engines to see what comes up. If you are getting sites that have some similarity to yours but aren't in the category you want to be in, keep looking for other terms. For example, you might pull up only direct competitors, sites that sell your product used, totally different sites, or even porn sites. Continue refining your list until you're satisfied you've identified the best keywords.

Create metatags   Once you have chosen your keywords, you will need to create metatags. Metatags are computer codes that contain hidden messages to search engine robots. These metatags will contain the keywords you've chosen and a description of your site, and can direct the robot to various pages within your site. A visitor cannot see your metatags. Unless experienced programmers are part of your design team, you will want to get some strategy and programming help with the metatags. Try searching within results for "Web page design" for metatags, or go to a site such as 123 Toolbox at

www.mcn.org/b/sitepromoter/123Exe/123/123PROMO/WORKSHOP
/metatag.html.

Submit your site to search engines   To submit your site to a search
engine, go to the engine, click on the button for "Submit Website,"
and follow the directions. When the site is up, check to see where it
comes up on the search engines; you may need to refine your keywords and resubmit.

Use other methods to attract visitors   In addition to the work you've
done to have your site turn up high on the list of search engine results,
you can do several other things to get people to visit your site.

* *Banner ads:* Banner ads are advertisements that appear on web pages,
  usually at the top, that are independent advertisements from a different
  company. Often, they are related to the topic of the web page, or their
  target audience is the same as the audience for the web page. Sites that
  offer free services, such as Bluelight.com (offers free ISP services) and
  Altavista.com (offers free web search services), often make money by
  selling banner ads on their sites. Also, smaller sites often exchange
  these ads with other sites (e.g., I'll show your ads if you'll show mine).

    The problem with exchanging banner ads with other sites is they are
  often visually distracting. Also, since your visitors can click on the
  banner ad and go to the advertiser's site, they provide visitors a channel off your site. So think carefully about your decision and be very
  choosy about the banner you include. If you decide to exchange banner ads, some free exchanges are:
  www.exchange-it.com
  www.4for5-banner-exchanges.com
  www.smartclicks.com
  www.4traffic.net

* *Web rings:* These are groups of sites that agree to form a ring of sites
  related to the same topic. At the bottom of the page for each site it says
  "Go to the next page in the web ring." Some rings are formally done
  through web sites and some are done informally. A problem with the
  informal rings is that if one page goes down, the ring is broken.

    Web rings offer you a way to gain visitors from sites with similar or
  related content, but they vary in quality and suitability. If you don't
  find a ring that's suitable, try creating your own. You'll benefit from traffic the other sites have pulled in. You will want some way to check
  traffic at your site and successful completions of any activities such as
  sales, donations, or requests for information. As you evaluate your

results, analyze how they relate to your purpose and focus on increasing traffic only if it is in line with your overall purpose. If you decide to join a web ring, a free service is www.webring.com.

- *Links:* You can ask other similar web sites to include a link to your page. Some sites have instructions that say, "Click here to add your site as a link." Others contact you and ask you to put a link to their page on your site. It is a good idea to ask permission to set up a link to another site. Often links are a reciprocal process, "I'll link to your site if you'll link to mine."

- *Advertising:* Consider advertising your site using other media. For instance, does a local radio station target the same audience as your site? Should you advertise in a trade magazine that's sent to the kind of people you want to visit your site?

Update your web site

- *How often?* Before you decide how often to update your web site, look back at your purpose and audience analysis. Some web sites quickly become outdated and useless if not updated, but other sites need little or no updating. Updating does encourage return visits, but if the information you're offering won't be affected, consider what you hope to achieve by changing the site and whether that achievement is in line with your goals and the needs of your audience.

- *How to evaluate?* Once your site is up and running, make periodic evaluations to see whether you are reaching your intended audience and fulfilling your purpose. Consider counting the number of hits and the number of purchases. Counting the number of visitors is easy using one of the many free **web counters.** Two sites that offer free web counters are www.hitbox.com and www.beseen.com.

Analyze the responses you get from visitors to determine whether you have successfully entered the web marketplace and created a site where visitors are having the conversations they and you both want.

Whether or not you plan to design a web site, this chapter will help you better understand the Internet by knowing the major steps involved in getting a successful site up and running.

CHAPTER 5 OUTLINE

I. COMPUTER-DESIGNED PRESENTATION AIDS
1. When to use computer-designed visuals
2. How to design your template
3. How to use multimedia design techniques
4. How to interact with computer-designed visuals

II. ELECTRONIC CONFERENCING
1. Videoconferencing
2. Electronic meeting systems (EMS)

III. TELEPHONES
1. Telephone guidelines
2. Voice mail guidelines
3. Conference call guidelines

CHAPTER 5

Electronic Tools for Oral Communication

M ost people in business engage in some form of electronic oral communication every day at work. You talk on the phone and listen to voice mail or answering machine messages. You watch presentations regularly. You may have a cell phone and, if you haven't already, will soon be participating in videoconferences or electronic meetings.

You probably already know that people form first impressions of you based on their first seven seconds of contact with you. When using electronic oral communication tools, the way you use the technology can tell others about your preparation, professionalism, and competence. This chapter will discuss the effective use of various types of electronic tools, including (1) multimedia presentation aids, (2) electronic conferencing, and (3) telephones.

I. COMPUTER-DESIGNED PRESENTATION AIDS

Effective visual aids are an important element of a successful presentation. One reason is that over a third of your audience is made up of visual learners, who learn best by seeing. But visual aids enhance learning for all audiences. Studies show that audiences will remember messages they see *and* hear more than twice as much as those they only see or only hear.

Since most people have become accustomed to television, MTV, and videos, you can have trouble holding audience attention unless you integrate computer-designed visuals into your presentations. Research shows that a presenter using computer-projected visuals scored 60 to 80 percent higher in the area of personal engagement and presenter effectiveness than the same presenter delivering the same information using overheads. The following sections will help you as you design and deliver multimedia presentations.

1. When to use computer-designed visuals

As a presenter you must decide when to use which type of visuals. Software programs such as Microsoft PowerPoint, Aldus Persuasion, and WordPerfect Presentations can help you design professional-looking visuals for your presentation. You can project these visuals on a computer projector or make them into transparencies for an overhead projector. In general, you can safely use computer-designed overhead transparencies instead of transparencies written by hand or on a word processor. However, in many cases, computer-projected visuals will look more professional and will give you more options than computer-designed transparencies.

Use computer-projected visuals when you:

- *Have a formal presentation.* If the format of your talk will be for you to present first and take questions second, projected visuals will work better than when the content will be variable depending on the audience interaction throughout.
- *Want to include sounds, short video clips, and active web links* as part of your presentation.

- *Need to make last-minute changes to your presentation.* You can make changes until the last minute before your presentation and your audience won't know.
- *Want to have a simultaneous web broadcast* of your presentation to receivers in other locations. Visuals can be included alone or in conjunction with a live video of the presenter.
- *Are trying to persuade your audience.* Research has shown that multimedia computer projection is particularly effective in persuasive presentations.
- *Want to save the expense* of making dozens of colored overheads that will be used only once.
- *Will be using videos too.* A projector can easily project from both a computer and a VCR. Most projectors have buttons to tell the machine which feed to use at a given time.
- *Must bring your own equipment with you.* If you will be traveling, and can afford it, you can now buy a smaller computer projector than overhead projector. LCD cameras can weigh under three pounds and be smaller than a standard day planner.
- *Want a high-quality projected image.* Often, detail is lost when your visual is printed onto an overhead transparency.

Do not use when you:

- *Will be facilitating a discussion,* using only a few visuals, and relying heavily on group input.
- *Need the room to be bright* and you do not have access to a projector that works effectively in a well-lit room.
- *Must write on the visual.* Although projected visuals can be modified in real time, in most cases it is easier and faster to use a marker on a transparency.
- *Cannot arrive a few minutes early,* cannot get help setting up, and don't have experience using the equipment.

The following section will help you design effective templates that can be displayed either as transparencies or as computer-projected visuals.

2. How to design your template

A template is a standard format for all of the slides in your presentation. The template you use determines the background design, the colors, and the overall look of your presentation. Every major presentation design program comes with many premade templates from which you can choose. Unfortunately, almost all of the premade templates are inappropriate for one reason or another. A common problem is that they do not provide adequate color contrast between the background color and font color. The following tips will help you as you design your template.

Choose a design that will match the formality of your presentation
Use a template that is appropriate for your audience. Select colors that match your audience and purpose. Colors such as blue and gray are more formal; pink and lime green are less formal. Choose fonts consistent with your theme.

More formal fonts

Arial, Times, **Antique Olive**, and Book Antique

Less formal fonts

Juice, Comic Sans, Matisse ITC , and *Brush Script*

Keep your slides simple, clean, and uncluttered   In general, your audience should be able to read your entire visual within 15 seconds. This means that most text lines should be fewer than eight words long and slides should be no more than five to seven lines long.

Be strategic in your placement of graphics   Studies show that people notice headings first and graphics second. Thus, the optimum place to put your graphics is in the lower right corner of your slide. This way, the slide will lead the viewer's eyes from the title, through the text, and over to the graphic.

Choose colors that will be visible from a distance when projected
In a darkened room, light text (e.g., white, yellow) on a medium-dark background (e.g., blue or forest green) will show up best. In a room with bright lights, or if using overheads, use a light background with dark (e.g., black, brown, navy) letters. Avoid using similar colors for both the font and the background. Most presentation design programs

will allow you to change the font and background color on all of the premade templates. If you cannot find a template you like with colors that provide contrast, changing the colors on an appropriate design is a good option.

Use font sizes and styles strategically   Choose fonts that can be read from a distance. Usually, 28-point font is large enough for an audience of twenty. Opt for easy-to-read fonts. Use large fonts for title slides and headings; use medium fonts for text; use smaller fonts for sources and references. You may want to use one style (sans serif) for headings, and another style (serif) for text, but do not use more than two or three different fonts lest your presentation look too busy and confusing.

Hard-to-read fonts

BeesKnees, *Brush Script*, **Impact,** and Curlz MT

Easy-to-read fonts

CG Times, Bookman Old Style, Arial, and Times New Roman

3. How to use multimedia design techniques

Use pictures and videos strategically   Many times, the adage "a picture is worth a thousand words" is equally true for presentation visuals. Furthermore, pictures will generally be more effective than words for the visual learners in your audience. Irrelevant graphics may distract the viewer.

Use sound clips strategically   Relevant music and noises can add refreshing interest and variety to a presentation. However, using distracting computer noises (such as gunshots or crashing sounds when bulleted points are presented) as part of your slide show may draw attention to the sound effects and not your content.

Use the animation functions to systematically disclose information   For example, you can reveal your ideas one at a time with the click of a mouse using the build function. By doing this, your audience will not be not distracted by reading your upcoming points on the slide before you get to them in your presentation. Likewise, it can be effective to display complex graphs and figures gradually so you can explain the elements as you add them to the slide. You can also have the program use a different color to highlight the point you're talking about, and/or to dim the points you've already covered.

Insert copies of your agenda slide to use as transitions in longer presentations   Make copies of your agenda slide and insert the copies between your major points. Highlight the appropriate point in each agenda copy by drawing a box around it, changing the color, or putting an arrow in front of it. This will show your audience where you are in the presentation.

Choose transition patterns carefully   Presentation design software allows you to choose from dozens of ways to transition from one slide to the next. For example, you can have the slide you have finished discussing slide down, spin away, wipe left, checkerboard away, or dissolve into the next slide. Beware, however, if you use too many different or creative transitions; they can distract from your content. The safest approach is to use one professional transition throughout your presentation.

Eliminate screen savers from the computer   Screen savers often include images that move and can distract your audience.

4. How to interact with computer-designed visuals
Having well-designed visuals is not enough. To make a successful presentation, you must use your visuals effectively while you present.

Practice your presentation   Practice with the equipment you will be using in the same room you will be presenting. Often colors look different when they are projected on a screen; give yourself time to adjust the colors. Decide which lights should be left on. Make sure the font is large enough to read. Bring your own equipment if practical. If not, make sure you are comfortable with the equipment before your presentation. One computer tip is to hit the "function" key and the "CRT/LCD" [often F8] key at the same time to toggle the image from computer screen to projector screen to both screens.

Practice forwarding your slides   If you are using a remote, know exactly where to point it. Know how to show previous slides using the remote. Do not fiddle with the remote. Do not use a remote that draws attention away from your presentation by working only part of the time. If you do not have a good remote, consider having a team member forward your slides for you.

Emphasize your main ideas Expand upon simple visuals and summarize complex visuals. Do not read every word on the screen. Instead, focus on the key points and discuss supporting details. For complex visuals, make sure your main idea is emphasized.

Look at your audience, not at the screen or the computer Keep the audience's focus on you as the presenter, not just on your slides. Maintain contact with your audience by adjusting the lights so you can be seen and you can see your audience. Use your laptop computer screen to skim your notes and face your audience at the same time.

Avoid showing work areas Leave the program in Slide Show view throughout your presentation. Practice navigating the program using keyboard controls so you can use your working screens and untidy, unprofessional work areas (e.g., outline view, slide sorter) as you design the presentation, not as you deliver it. Place a blank screen at the end of your presentation so you will have a nondistracting slide to display during your question and answer period.

Have a backup plan Electronic equipment often fails due to compatibility problems, viruses, and lack of technical support. Even if you test your equipment immediately before your presentation, you may have a failure during your presentation. Overhead copies of your slides are one good option for backups.

For additional information about multimedia presentation aids, consult one of the web sites listed below:

- *www.creativemindsinc.com:* Offers background templates, tips for effective presentations, and an online presentation magazine.
- *www.presentations.com:* Provides tips on using projectors, clip art, and multimedia business cards.
- *www.presentersuniversity.com:* Offers free downloads of background templates, gives helpful tips, and provides "ask the professor," a forum for you to ask questions and get expert advice.
- *www.powerpointers.com:* Gives general advice about planning and building an effective presentation, as well as specific advice for trainers, negotiators, sales representatives, educators, and interviewers.

II. ELECTRONIC CONFERENCING

In addition to face-to-face oral communication, you will have many opportunities to engage in other types of oral communication. The purpose of this section is to discuss two types of communication technology that can be used in oral communication. The first part discusses videoconferencing and the second part discusses electronic meeting systems. Videoconferences show pictures of meeting participants who are in remote locations. Electronic meeting software is generally used to facilitate group meetings using words only, but can also be used in conjunction with videoconferences.

1. Videoconferencing

Videoconferencing is a way for people in diverse locations to simultaneously see and talk to other people. The cost of installing videoconferencing systems has dropped dramatically in the last few years. Experts predict that sales of these group systems will more than triple in the next three years.

What videoconferencing is   You will probably use one of the two common types of videoconferencing equipment.

- *Room systems:* Room systems are permanently set up in a dedicated room. The room is generally equipped with a large screen at the front that shows the participants in the other location(s). These systems use special cameras, hardware, and high-speed Integrated Services Digital Network (ISDN) lines.

- *Desktop systems:* Participants use individual desktop computers, usually in their offices. Each computer has videoconferencing software and a webcam (web camera). Desktop systems use local area network (LAN) lines or regular telephone lines and generally transmit the images over the web. Because of the decreased bandwidth, these systems are often more jerky than room systems. Also, the resolution and bandwidth is not adequate to show fine detail, such as writing on a white board. However, because they are only a fraction of the cost of room systems, they can be an attractive alternative. Also, desktop systems are good for geographically dispersed employees in small offices without conference rooms.

When to use videoconferencing   Videoconferencing works well when:

- *You need the benefit of face-to-face contact* and want to save the time and expense associated with traveling to another location.
- *Your goal is to provide information,* such as explaining or training.
- *You are broadcasting presentations* and talks to many employees.

When to avoid video conferencing   Videoconferencing does not work as well when:

- *The time lag difficulties will be distracting* or detrimental to the communication.
- *The added social context of face-to-face communication is needed.* For example, if the group members have never met, consider a face-to-face meeting because videoconferences are not as good for developing rapport.
- *The success of your meeting relies on short bursts of input* from all participants. In videoconferences, comments are generally longer and come from fewer people.
- *The group must discuss sensitive issues.* Sometimes participants will be more honest and perceptive if meeting face to face.
- *The group misses out on the side discussions* that often result in creative new ideas during a face-to-face meeting.

How to use videoconferencing   The following lists provide suggestions for the leader of the videoconference and for all participants.

If you are the leader, before the videoconference you should:

- *Plan everything in advance.* Don't waste participants' time and don't waste company money on unnecessary and expensive line charges. Prioritize topics.
- *Distribute agendas, reports, or visuals* to all participants one week before the videoconference.
- *Appoint leaders for each site.* Generally, a videoconference has one leader for the whole conference, and additional secondary leaders at each site. The rest of the suggestions apply to all leaders.
- *Arrive at the videoconference location early.* Make sure all equipment is working properly.

- *Test your graphics.* Most systems have document cameras. Many systems can also transmit documents from computers. Make sure you don't lose too much resolution during the transmission and that the image is clear to those in other locations.
- *Program your cameras in advance.* For example, you can set the camera to start with a wide-angle view of everyone in the room, and have a zoom-in shot of the first presenter ready as the second view. Preset the cameras/keypad with several views and your conference will look more polished.

Before a videoconference, all participants should:

- *Choose clothing carefully.* Avoid plaids, prints, patterns, and all white clothes. Also, avoid wearing black and red because those colors can appear to bleed on the screen. Good color choices are blue, green, and purple. Wear contact lenses or nonglare glasses.
- *Come prepared.* Know what's on the agenda and bring relevant supporting materials.
- *Come early.* Practice using your keypad so you'll be prepared when the meeting starts.

During the videoconference, the leader should:

- *Begin and end on time.*
- *Have participants introduce themselves* at the beginning of the videoconference.
- *Show the agenda* using the document camera at the beginning of the videoconference.
- *Keep all participants on track.* Discourage participants who dominate the conversation unnecessarily.
- *Ask for input* from reticent group members. Since their pictures often won't show unless they talk, the group can forget that important employees are participating.

During the videoconference, all participants should:

- *Look at the camera* when you want to talk to someone in another location. Do not look at the person's picture on your screen.
- *Avoid moving around* when someone else is talking. Side conversations and movements can be distracting to the other participants.
- *Use the mute function* if you must talk to someone in the room or cough.

It's a good idea to use the mute when you are not talking to the group because videoconferencing systems are generally voice activated.

- *Avoid eating.* Even if you use the mute feature, it doesn't look professional to eat in front of others who are not eating.

- *Speak naturally and be yourself.* Pretend that the other participants are sitting in the room with you.

2. Electronic meeting systems (EMS)

Electronic meeting technology is used both in videoconferences and in traditional face-to-face meetings. Also called electronic meeting software, EMS, and meetingware, this software facilitates meetings by networking the computers and allowing equal input from all members of the group. All participants are involved at the same time and are allowed equal input. Meetingware is generally used alone, in a written-only format, but can be used in conjunction with face-to-face meetings that also use oral communication.

What EMS is   Electronic meetings are led by trained facilitators who control the group discussion. Group members can participate from workstations in their offices or from terminals (with a keyboard and screen) in a conference room set up for an electronic meeting. Generally, all of the group activities—including brainstorming and recording ideas, organizing and analyzing alternatives, making and responding to suggestions, ranking and voting on choices, planning for implementation of the decision, and writing the minutes—are done in writing at the time of the meeting.

When to use EMS   The benefits of electronic meeting technology are that it:

- Keeps discussions on track
- Engages the participants
- Allows all participants to contribute and vote at the same time
- Analyzes the voting results
- Provides a written record of the meeting
- Speeds the pace of meetings
- Increases participation from employees at all levels; decreases impact of hierarchy

- Works well when soliciting input from all participants of a large group

Do not use EMS when:

- Trying to build rapport and emotional ties
- Increased anonymity and honesty will cause problems

How to use EMS   A facilitator organizes the sessions and input. The participants' responses and suggestions are displayed on a screen at the front of the room or on the individual computer screens. All participants should be prepared to engage in candid, rapid-fire discussions. Depending on the system the company is running, the facilitator can choose to use the technology in many ways. The facilitator can direct the group to brainstorm ideas or to respond to various proposals. For example, if the leader wants to know how the group is feeling on an issue, an anonymous straw poll can be taken. Sometimes, everyone in the group is in agreement without even discussing the matter much.

III. TELEPHONES

Because telephones are used so widely, your ability to use them effectively can make or break your career. The first section below gives
general phone use advice that can be applied to telephones, voice mail,
and cell phones. Sections two and three give information specific to
voice mail and conference calls.

1. Telephone guidelines

The telephone, although not seen as high-tech, is still one of the most
commonly used electronic communication devices. The following sections offer tips on telephone use.

When talking on the phone, do:

- *Make your own calls:* Having a secretary place the call and then letting
  you know when the person is on the line can be seen as rude unless
  you're in a very high, executive-level position.
- *Be prepared:* Create an outline of your objectives and questions about
  the topic of the call.
- *Remain focused during the phone call:* Take notes, outline important
  points, then summarize what you hear back to the other party.
- *Use effective vocal cues:* Sound alert; speak distinctly and directly into
  the mouthpiece.
- *Smile.* Your listener can tell the difference. Sound pleasant.
- *Speak slowly* enough to be understood.
- *Identify yourself* at the beginning of the call.
- *Be ready* to leave a message if necessary.
- *Introduce others* listening in on the call.
- *Call back* if you place a call that becomes disconnected, no matter
  whose fault it is.
- *Answer your phone quickly,* within a few rings; identify yourself at the
  beginning of the call; acknowledge caller by name to personalize the
  conversation.

When talking on the phone, don't:

- *Eat or drink.*
- *Multitask* (e.g., open mail or talk to others who are not part of the call)
- *Call after business hours.*
- *Use a speakerphone* if you share an office or if it's difficult to hear you because you sound like you're in a cave.
- *Ignore the first caller* when answering call waiting.

When talking on a cell phone, don't:

- *Use a cell phone in enclosed public spaces,* such as theaters, churches, concerts, courtrooms, lunch and dinner appointments, and places where people go to relax.
- *Forget that the call is not private* when others are around; remember that others can hear you.
- *Leave the ringer turned on.* If you must keep your cell phone on at all times, switch the ringer to vibrating or silent mode when you are in a place where the ringing might bother others.

2. Voice mail guidelines

Research shows that your chance of reaching a businessperson on the first call is only 17 percent. Statistically, you're more likely to reach a voice mail machine. These systems are also called "phone mail" and "voice messaging."

Advantages

- *Allows people to conduct business* during different work schedules and time zones.
- *Allows people to contact* a person who is hard to contact.
- *Delivers the message* directly to the person for whom it is intended.
- *Allows easy access* to messages.
- *Add comments and forward messages* to others easily.
- *Send the same message* to multiple recipients easily.

Disadvantages

- *Caller cannot get through* to an operator.
- *In-house resistance;* some people dislike using or talking to a machine

How to use voice mail   Here are some techniques for leaving effective voice mail messages for others.

- *Speak distinctly and loudly* enough to be easily heard.
- *Identify yourself.* Usually this means giving your first and last name, title, and company name.
- *Give the time and date you are calling,* unless you know the machine gives time and date.
- *Leave your complete telephone number* at the beginning and the end of the message. Even if the recipient has your number, this makes it easier to call you back.
- *Keep the message well organized, short, and clear.* While you are explaining the reason for your call, be succinct, informative, and action oriented. Avoid rambling.
- *Be positive sounding.* Edit out negatives.
- *Be businesslike and professional.* Avoid filler words such as "um" and "ah," and sounding tentative.
- *Edit your message.* After you have created your message, listen to it, and edit it if necessary. Does your message sound clear? Are you speaking slowly enough? Is the message specific and precise?
- *Remember that your message can be forwarded.* Be professional, even when leaving messages for friends.

Your colleagues' impressions of you will also be affected by how you return messages.

- *Either reply, forward, or delete the message.* Don't just save and ignore the message. Creating a backlog of voice mail will only complicate your life. By being prompt when returning messages, you will be more efficient in the work you do.
- *Return the call promptly.* Reply the same day the message was received, or as soon as is possible.
- *If you are unable to provide an answer,* return the call to let sender know you received the message. If possible, include a progress report.

- *Avoid telephone tag.* If you have trouble reaching someone, give additional information to reduce phone tag time. For example, if you know the person you are calling well, you may want to propose three different proposed meeting times and ask if any would be convenient. If you do not know the person, you may want to list the times you will be at your desk to take a call.

3. Conference call guidelines

Conference calls are telephone conversations in which more than two people are involved in the discussion. Many times, colleagues do not have time to travel to meet in person or to set up an electronic conference, but want to solicit input from several people at the same time. Conference calls can provide a quick, inexpensive solution.

Advantages

- *Allow for simultaneous participation* from people in various locations.
- *Fast and easy to set up;* technology failures are unlikely.
- Inexpensive to conduct and saves time and expense related to travel.

Disadvantages

- *Visual and tactile aspects* of the communication are lost.
- *Difficult to establish rapport* and to persuade, and
- *May be dominated* by aggressive, vocal participants.

How to participate in conference calls

Before the call:

- *Inform all participants* about the day, time, duration, and purpose of the call.
- *Provide printed agendas* and information relevant to the call.
- *Call from a quiet location.*

During the call, the leader should:

- *Introduce all participants* at the beginning of the call.
- *Make sure all participants are close to speakers* and can hear and be heard.

- *Begin by reviewing the agenda* and purpose for the meeting.
- *Encourage reticent participants* to contribute their views.

During the call, all participants should:

- *Speak clearly and identify yourself* if other participants can't identify you by your voice.
- *Direct your questions* to specific people or offices.
- *Pause regularly* so others can comment.
- *Allow others to finish their comments* before speaking.
- *Avoid using cell phones* because of poor sound quality.

The way you use oral communication technology affects your reputation at work. The tips in this chapter are designed to help you make a good impression on others.

CHAPTER 6 OUTLINE

I. HOW TO DESIGN AN ELECTRONIC RÉSUMÉ
1. Effective résumé design
2. Effective use of keywords
3. Effective distribution

II. HOW TO USE THE WEB IN YOUR JOB SEARCH
1. Post your résumé on the web
2. Post your résumé on job boards
3. Search for job-related information on the web

CHAPTER 6

Electronic Tools for Job Searches

Every year, more and more companies are using electronic media to find prospective employees. A survey by KPMG Peat Marwick found that over half of large companies use applicant-tracking systems. New technology is making it easier for employers to find and compare candidates. A computer can screen hundreds of résumés in a matter of seconds; it would take an employee hours to read and compare all of the résumés.

Advantages of using electronic media in your job search include:

- *Bias-free screening:* Your résumé will be more likely to be screened by a bias-free computer rather than by a human.
- *Wide distribution:* You can quickly, easily, and inexpensively distribute your résumé nationwide to hundreds of employers.
- *You can apply in one office of a multinational company,* and have your résumé considered by hundreds of international affiliates.
- *You can be considered for a variety of positions* for which you are qualified.

Disadvantages to using electronic media in your job search include:

- *Most people still find their jobs based on personal contacts.* You may waste a great deal of time online.
- *If you do not use the appropriate keywords, you may be overlooked* for a job you are qualified for.
- *Résumé management systems exclude all but the top matches.*

The following sections will tell you (1) how to design and distribute an electronic résumé and (2) how to use the web in your job search.

I. HOW TO DESIGN AN ELECTRONIC RÉSUMÉ

The résumé is still your most important job search document; it is a major factor in the hiring decision for 90 percent of new hires. Since more and more candidates are being screened by computers, it is a good idea to have a résumé that can be read by both a computer and a human.

Most job seekers can design one résumé that is both pleasing for a human to look at and scannable for a computer. Scanners and databases have become good at reading bold, italics, many types of font styles, and other special types of lettering. Since you may not know whether the company will scan your résumé, this can be an effective approach. However, some job seekers in creative areas such as advertising, theater, and marketing, may want one fancy résumé for hardcopy distribution that uses vertical text, columns, and/or unusual fonts—as well as a more simple, scannable résumé. The first part of this section gives tips for effective résumé design.

The second section helps you to think in terms of keywords and hits. Computers fill job positions by looking for résumés that match words that describe job skills or requirements. When writing your résumé, consider the number of words you include that will match job descriptors. The third section provides suggestions for successfully distributing your résumé.

1. Effective résumé design

The following tips will help you design a résumé that will be effective when read by either a human or a computer.

Put your name first and address second at the top of your résumé
Some computers look for this information at the top of the résumé and put it automatically into a profile sheet. Having two addresses, such as home address on the left margin and school address on the right margin, can confuse some computers.

Include your email address   More and more companies are using email to stay in touch with applicants. Use a personal email address and check your mail regularly. Do not include an unprofessional (e.g., too cute or silly) email alias that will discourage companies. The inclusion of an email address also signals that you have some computer savvy; people who use email are seen as likely to have other high-tech abilities.

Avoid complex résumé layouts, tables, and graphics Scanners often have trouble reading résumés that look like newspapers or brochures. Do not use columns or unusual organization patterns. Scanners work well when reading text, but often get confused when looking at pictures and figures.

Do not use vertical lettering Although a human can easily read vertical words, such as your name and address running vertically along the left margin, this will often cause the computer to have trouble reading your résumé.

Use simple fonts that can be read by a computer Do not use fancy or unusual fonts such as *Kaufmann* and *Minstral*; many scanners have trouble with unusual and stylistic fonts. Although most scanners can read traditional serif fonts such as Times Roman and Garamond, some scanners have an easier time reading sans serif fonts such as Verdana or Arial. Do not use shaded letters or anything smaller than a 10-point font or larger than a 14-point font.

2. Effective use of keywords

A 1998 study by Baker, DeTienne, and Smart showed that two-thirds of the *Fortune* 500 companies either have or are planning to implement electronic applicant tracking systems. These systems, also called electronic résumé management systems, match applicants with job openings. They use résumé scanning hardware and software to input résumés and they use computer equipment to match those résumés to hiring needs. To match the applicants and positions, an employee at the company or job placement firm types in a keyword search and the computer returns a list of qualified applicants.

Applicant tracking systems use keywords to find potential employees. When managers and human resource employees want to fill positions using an applicant tracking system, they look for employees whose résumés closely match the job requirements by using keywords that describe the requisite experience, education, certifications, and skills. After the employee keys in the search, the computer returns a list of applicants who match the criteria, generally with a ranking from best to worst and a percentage beside each candidate (e.g., a 100 percent or 65 percent keyword match). Since the computers are looking for specific keywords, a résumé that says "I have never programmed in HTML or C++" will get more hits than a résumé that says "I empowered 1,200 employees."

Think in terms of keywords when you write your résumé   Use a pen to highlight potential keywords on a hard copy of your résumé. Look at the highlighted words and ask yourself, "Do these words accurately describe my qualifications?" If you are responding to an ad, make sure you're using the job title and keyword descriptors mentioned in the ad.

Include plenty of nouns   Use nouns that describe your degrees, job titles, departments, certifications, computer skills, and other qualifications. Traditionally, the focus in résumé writing was on using action verbs. Although these are still important to include, computers generally look for the nouns that describe specific qualifications. If you have trouble including keywords, consult the help wanted ads of a

EXAMPLES OF KEYWORDS

MBA	Advertising
CPA	Payroll
ADA	Benefits
BS	Accounts Payable
BA	Marketing
C++	Compensation
JIT	ISO 9000
ICU	Counseling
HTML	Training
IEEE	Dosimetry
CAD	Bronchoscopy

major newspaper or web site to look for appropriate keywords that describe your skills and qualifications.

Use standard abbreviations and jargon   Include words that are widely used in your field, even if the words may be unfamiliar to those in other fields. Make sure the words and abbreviations are spelled correctly or they will not be recognized.

List your professional organizations   The names and acronyms for professional associations are often used as keywords in job searches.

List your computer skills   Companies often want employees who have specific computer skills, even when hiring for a nontechnical job. For example, include word processing and spreadsheet programs as well as job-specific software programs you are able to use.

Include a skills section if needed   If you're having trouble including keywords in your résumé, consider adding a skills section. For example, if you've taken software or programming classes but haven't earned a computer science degree or had a chance to use the skills in previous jobs, you can list them in this section.

3. Effective distribution

Once you've designed the perfect résumé, it's time to send it to prospective employers. The following tips will help you avoid difficulties when electronic tools are involved in your job search and when you want your paper résumé to be easily scannable.

Print in black ink on light-colored, 8 1/2″ × 11″ paper   Do not use darker or marbled paper, because the scanner relies on the contrast between the background and font to read the text. Print on one side only, because the ink from the other side can show through and because a human may not notice or scan the information on the back side.

Include a cover letter   Many firms scan, store, and search for keywords in cover letters as well as résumés. Even if they don't use the letter for keywords, most firms read the letters when deciding which candidates to interview.

Send original, unfolded copies of your résumé   Scanners may have trouble reading ink dots left by copy machines and important words in the creases of your folds. Use a laser printer if you can; the sharper your résumé, the more professional it looks and the easier it is for the computer to read.

Do not staple your résumé and/or cover letter   If the staple is left in the paper, the scanner may read it as an "I." Even if the staple is removed, the pages will be more likely to stick together when going through the scanner.

Do not send multiple résumés to a company that uses an electronic résumé management system   Before computerized applicant tracking systems, you could apply to one department with a résumé that said you were an internal auditor and to another department with a résumé that said you were a general accountant. Now, if the system pulls up two different résumés, it can look like you're not focused or not honest.

Use caution when sending your résumé electronically If you are sending your résumé via email, electronic submission, or online job boards, remember that many fonts do not transfer well and some formatting may be lost. If you paste your résumé and/or cover letter into the text of an email, always proofread before sending. If you send your résumé as an attachment, use a common word processing program such as MS Word, and send one formatted copy and one basic copy using text, *rich text format (.rtf), or ASCII.*

II. HOW TO USE THE WEB IN YOUR JOB SEARCH

The digital age is also affecting job search techniques. New job search tools are available to help employers find you and to help you find the right job. In the last section, we looked at techniques for designing an electronic résumé. The purpose of this section is to examine some of the ways you can use the web in your job search.

I. Post your résumé on the web

More and more job seekers are posting their résumés on the web. In addition to posting your resume in databases, you can create your own home page, independent of any job board. Stories abound of recruiters who wake up early every day to search the web for job seekers who have recently posted résumé web pages. You can create your own web space, outline your qualifications, and provide evidence of your abilities and accomplishments. By listing the URL for your web-based résumé on your paper résumé and including it in your online job applications, you give employers an additional avenue for learning more about your qualifications.

Design your home page and the rest of the site to work as a whole
The home page is like a table of contents for the site and is the most important consideration. Your first screen will create the reader's first impression of you. Put your most important points on your first screen. Do not expect readers to scroll or look past the initial screen if they are not impressed. Design the home page so it presents your employment objective and main qualifications in a clear, uncluttered fashion.

Use effective layout and design techniques, even if you are not looking for computer-related work The primary difference between printed or scannable résumés and web résumés is the layout and design. Include *hyperlinks* and *hypertextuality* on your home page and throughout the site to make your web-based résumé more detailed and descriptive than a hard copy résumé.

Include keywords Using appropriate, descriptive nouns as discussed in the previous section, is also critical when using the web in your job search, whether you're posting your résumé on a web site or in a database.

Provide clear hyperlinks to evidence of your abilities and accomplishments   For example, your education section can include a link to a scanned copy of your grade transcripts that lists all of the classes you've taken. Your experience section can have links to a portfolio of your work, web pages you've designed, papers you've written, and/or software you've programmed. Your activities and honors section can have a link to a newspaper article that reports your receiving an award or recognition.

Include links to more detailed information about your work experience   For instance, you may want to have one screen that lists your past employment. This way, potential employers can see your experience in one glance. However, to keep it to one screen, you'll probably need to limit your job descriptions. To provide the details you can make a link for each of your past jobs that provides in-depth information such as other jobs you performed while your co-workers were on vacation and additional skills you learned.

Focus on displayed pages, not printed pages   The traditional advice to limit your résumé to one or two pages does not hold true with online résumés. Instead, think in terms of what can be displayed in one screen. Provide clear links so the reader can effortlessly "channel surf" to other interesting pages.

Match your résumé web site style to the position and type of company   Different jobs require different résumé approaches. For example, if you wanted to be a financial analyst for a large, traditional, conservative organization, your résumé should look less creative than if you wanted to be an ad designer for a small, trendy public relations firm.

Consider privacy issues when deciding what to post   If you post your résumé online, it will be available to millions of people. You may or may not want your name, address, and personal information distributed this widely. For example, if you do not want your current employer to find your résumé on the web, you may want to provide a "mail to" line through which potential employers can contact you. You can either set up your own personal employment email account or use one of the message services offered by commercial employ-ment agencies.

2. Post your résumé on job boards

Job boards can be effective places to look for jobs, particularly for those in technical fields. Job boards are web sites that list job seekers and/or job openings. A survey of 525 job seekers found that job can-didates who used the Internet to look for jobs found more than five job leads each and they secured more than one interview each.

The following sections describe some of the popular job boards and job sites. Although they've been categorized for your convenience, many of the sites really fall into several categories, serve many different audiences, and provide a great deal of information. Policies and fees vary from company to company; carefully read this information before choosing which one(s) to use. Use the bookmark feature of your browser to keep a record of job boards that look promising.

General job boards

- *www.careerbuilder.com:* Allows you to search for job by industry, com-pany, and location. You may post your résumé and follow links to other sites with career advice.
- *www.jobtrak.com:* Has listings for various types of jobs, including full-time jobs, part-time jobs, and internships. Also includes information about job fairs, recruiters, résumés, and cover letters.
- *www.nationjob.com:* Is divided into categories: job seekers and employers. Features free email, links to other web sites, and community discussions.

Job boards for university students and recent graduates

- *www.careermosaic.com:* Contains a college connection section as well as an online job fair, a career resource center, and many other helpful tools. Has over 250,000 job postings.
- *www.hotjobs.com:* Allows job seekers to search by keyword, company, or location. More than 6,000 companies use this site to find applicants. Is organized by industry.
- *www.jobdirect.com:* Is a helpful site for students who are looking for internships, summer jobs, or entry-level career positions.
- *www.jobweb.org:* Has partnered with hundreds of colleges and univer-

sities to provide online job resources for undergraduate and graduate students.

Job boards for MBAs and executive-level employees

- *www.espan.com:* Offers both job search information and job listings. The motto for this interactive employment network is "the right person for the job and the right job for the person."
- *www.dice.com:* Includes Information Technology job listings and career and salary information. Great for the techno-MBA.
- *www.occ.com,* also called *www.monster.com:* Contains over 450,000 job listings. This popular site also has helpful advice on careers, salaries, cost of living, and other topics.

Job boards for government jobs

- *www.ajb.dni.us:* Provides information about the public employment service; lists over 500,000 jobs. This is America's Job Bank, run by the Labor Department.
- *www.usajobs.opm.gov:* Lists current government job openings and provides online applications. This is the U.S. government's official job site.
- *www.whitehouse.gov:* Includes information about jobs as White House fellows and interns.

Newspaper job listing sites

- *www.careerpath.com:* Provides access to jobs from the *Boston Globe, Chicago Tribune, Los Angeles Times, New York Times, San Jose Mercury,* and the *Washington Post.*
- *www.usatoday.com:* Posts the help wanted ads from *USA Today.*
- *www.JobAdsUSA.com:* Is a national database of classified ad listings.

Multiple job board search sites

- *www.yep.com:* Includes links to over 600 other employment sites. Search under "business" and then "employment."
- *www.flipdog.com:* Contains over 650,000 jobs. An excellent search engine.

- *www.Job-search-engine.com:* Allows you to search as many as 10 boards using the same group of keywords and job parameters.

Recruiter sites

- *www.headhunter.net:* Includes access to free job listings and free career advice. Allows you to search over 250,000 jobs organized by profession. Merged with CareerMosaic in 2000.
- *www.recruitersonline.com:* Is a global community of headhunters and recruiters. Job seekers can post résumés and can locate recruiters appropriate for their employment searches.

The following suggestions will help you as you use job boards in your job search.

Check policies before posting your résumé   Check job board policies before you post your résumé. For example, recruiters who work on contingency get paid only when someone they refer is hired for a job. Sometimes, these recruiters search databases for qualified applicants and respond to hundreds of want ads for them without asking. In addition, a recruiter's high fee may discourage a company from considering your résumé.

Do not rely solely on computer contact   Don't expect companies to open and read your email attachments, such as your résumé. When in doubt, send a hard copy of your résumé and application materials via postal mail or fax.

Try to schedule an in-person interview when you can   Computer contact cannot replace human contact. Generally, you will not be offered a job until the company has had a chance to meet you in person.

Realize that online job searches work better for some types of jobs
Many computer and technical companies use electronic media to look for candidates. Companies that do not rely on computers as much and businesses looking for liberal arts and humanities candidates often do not use computers to look for employees.

3. Search for job-related information on the web

In addition to advertising yourself online, you can use the following resources to look for job-related information on the web. The following sections will describe sites offering career advice, salary information, electronic résumé advice, job listings, and company information.

Sites offering career advice

- *www.careermag.com:* Includes an online magazine that archives articles about interviewing, résumé writing, and other helpful advice.

- *www.jobtrak.com:* Lists helpful information about résumé development, cover letters, and other aspects of the job search.

- *www.dbm.com/jobguide:* Has useful job search advice on using the Internet, writing résumés and cover letters, and online application procedures.

- *www.futurestep.com:* Is maintained by the well-respected firm, Korn-Ferry. It creates a profile, crosses it against its opportunities, and provides a number of avenues to explore.

- *www.careers.wsj.com:* Offers high-quality and up-to-date career advice for business professionals.

- *www.asktheheadhunter.com:* Provides a great deal of practical commentary on such topics as résumés, salary negotiation, and interviews.

Sites offering salary information

- *www.homefair.com/homefair/cmr/salcalc.html:* Provides a salary calculator so you can compare cost-of-living expenses for various areas.

- *www.stats.bls.gov* Includes information about market trends and salaries. Maintained by the U.S. Bureau of Labor Statistics.

- *www.hotjobs.com:* Contains a salary wizard that helps you to find the appropriate pay range for your skills, as well as listing job postings for students and professionals.

Sites offering electronic résumé advice

- *www.wired-resumes.com:* Provides all the tools and resources needed for you to create and post an online résumé.

- *www.tripod.com:* Offers everything you need to develop an online résumé. Free and easy to use, this site also provides free web hosting services up to 50 MB.

Other sites that include job listings   Use keywords when you visit sites so you can narrow the search from 800,000 general jobs to 40 jobs that match your qualifications.

- *Any major search engine* (e.g., AOL, CompuServe, MSN, Yahoo!) can be used to access the help wanted ads from major newspapers throughout the country.
- *Help wanted ads* are often placed in professional newsgroups and web sites.
- *A company's web site* will often list job openings and is a good place to go to look for positions you're interested in and qualified for.

Sites about companies   Find out more about the company and what it does before you go to a scheduled interview. Several web sites are available that list specific information about a variety of companies:

- *www.companysleuth.com:* Searches overnight for information on the companies you specify.
- *www.prnewswire.com:* and *www.business-wire.com:* Contain press releases and company news information.
- *Company's web site:* At a minimum, you should know what is on a company's own web site before you go in for an interview.

The suggestions in this chapter will help you to successfully use electronic media in your job search.

E-GLOSSARY

Throughout this book, potentially confusing terms are set in bold italics. Those words, along with selected other commonly used technical words are defined in this glossary.

Agents: Also known as web agents, or intelligent software agents. Little programs that are sent over the web to run on another computer. These programs do tasks such as intelligently gather data, or display animations.

ASCII: (American Standard Code for Information Interchange), pronounced "asskey." This code assigns numbers to 256 characters, such as those found on a common keyboard, plus some lines and Greek characters. The common colloquial use means just the human readable text, without graphics or html codes. For example, "Send me your report in ASCII" would mean to save it as text and send it, so no pictures or formatting codes would be embedded.

Attachments: Separate files you include with your email message. These files are usually created in a specific format, such as MS Word or Excel. Beware: attachments may carry viruses.

B2B (**B**usiness to **B**usiness): Internet services aimed at facilitating communications or transactions between businesses, rather than directly to the end user.

Banner ads: Ads appearing at the top or bottom of a web page, usually placed there by the hosting service rather than the creator of the web page.

BBS (**B**ulletin **B**oard **S**ystem): The electronic analog to the pins-and-cork bulletin board, where messages and ads can be posted for anyone to read. A computer system that allows users to log in, exchange messages, and download programs. The Bulletin Board is where the messages are posted to be read.

Bitmap files: The raw, number computer representation of an image. The most common example is the .bmp picture format. The downside of a bitmap representation is it tends to be large. A compressed standard, such as JPEG (.jpg) will store an image in much less space. (See page 60.)

Boolean operators: Allows for more focused web searches on some search engines. Look for a button that says "advanced search" or "search options." Common Boolean operators are *and, or, and not* and *not.* For example, *Website and Awards* would only find pages with both of the words *Website* and *Award.* It is noteworthy the words do not need to appear side-by-side in the site. *Video Conferencing or Videoconferencing* would find web pages with either or both of the words "Video Conferencing" *or* "Videoconferencing." (See page 19.)

Browsers: A program that allows users to find and access documents from anywhere on the web. Popular browsers are Netscape and Microsoft Internet Explorer.

Chat room: An electronic forum in which multi-users can "talk" with each other about any topic in real time. Usually the messages are typed, but some chat rooms permit the sending of pretyped messages, sounds, and images. (See pages 43–47.)

Clip art: Library of images available to put in documents, presentations, or web pages.

Cookie: Information saved on your computer as a result of visiting a web site (e.g., the time of your last visit and where you have browsed). Never visit a site on a work computer you would be embarrassed to have your boss know about, as a cookie may tell your boss about where you have been. Any web site can see any cookie. Most browsers allow you to reject cookies, but then some web pages will not work. (See page 8.)

Discussion forum: Electronically, these forums are usually hosted by USENET groups, web sites, or email lists.

DjVu technology: Image compression standard, optimized for scanned images.

Domain: A group of networked computers that share a common communications address in a convenient readable form such as Internet, email, or Telnet.

Domain name: A domain name is part of a URL; usually positioned after a period and consists of two or three letters such as .com, .org, .edu, or .gov.

Download: To get information from a remote computer to your local computer.

E: The prefix *E* means *electronic;* for example, ebusiness, email, etc.

E-business: Any business conducted primarily via electronic means, usually using the World Wide Web, but sometimes also used to refer to business via fax, phone, and computer. (See pages 3–11.)

E-commerce: Buying and selling electronically, usually via the web.

E-communication: Electronic communication: the transfer of meaning between humans assisted by technology or electronic media, such as by email. (See pages 3–11.)

Emoticons: Typewritten symbols for a facial expression or a human emotion, often used in email. An example is this smiley : -), which looks like a smiley face when viewed sideways. (See page 37.)

Encryption: A method of converting information into a code so the data is inaccessible to unauthorized users. Intended users then decrypt data using a password, making information readable. *Caution:* Some encryptions are export controlled, so care needs to be taken when sending encrypted information to foreign countries.

Extranet: A web-based computer network designed to facilitate communication between a company and its suppliers, customers, joint venture partners, and others outside the organization. (See pages 25–26.)

FAQ (**F**requently **A**sked **Q**uestions): A compilation of commonly asked questions and answers usually intended for newcomers. Often posted by newsgroups and email lists.

Firewall: A computer, usually a server, through which all Internet communications must pass. This helps prevent unauthorized access to a company's computers. Can also refer to a computer program, on a single computer, that blocks unauthorized access.

Flaming: An offensive, rude, or angry message sent electronically. (See pages 37 and 47.)

FTP (**F**ile **T**ransfer **P**rotocol): A method for transferring files over a network. On the web, this often occurs transparently.

FTP.SSH (**F**ile **T**ransfer **P**rotocol **S**ecure **SH**ell): An easy-to-use, secure method of transferring files online, like SFTP (Secure FTP).

GIF (**G**raphics **I**nterchange **F**ormat) files: File format used to store images electronically. GIF is the most common format for storing images on the web. (See page 61.)

Hit: Whenever a web page is visited. Web traffic is often reported as the number of hits, or hits per month. (See page 19.)

Home page: The first screen or main page of a web site, the home page contains an introduction to the organization or person, plus hyperlinks to other sections of the web site. (See pages 57–58.)

Host: The service that provides the computers and maintenance for web sites or other electronic services. Examples of hosting services include www.NBCi.com and www.geocities.com. Hundreds of hosting services are listed at www.tophosts.com. (See page 66.)

HTML (**H**yper**T**ext **M**arkup **L**anguage): The computer system used to format text and images, and to set up hyperlinks between documents. Used extensively in making web pages, and increasingly popular for use in email and documentation. See also **XML**.

HTTP (**HyperText Transfer Protocol**): Standard method of publishing information as hypertext in HTML; a protocol used on the web to govern transfer of data between the client and server.

HTTPS: A secure version of HTTP.

Hyperlink: Cross-reference that takes you to a related document or another location within the same document. Links are usually formatted using a different font, style, or color (typically blue).

Hypertext: see HTML. (See page 95.)

I: Prefix meaning *Internet,* for example *i-business.*

Infomediary: A third-party trustee or broker for information. For example, an infomediary might be used to contact someone electronically yet anonymously. Another example could be a business that will advertise on behalf of another business, to a customer base for a fee. (See page 8.)

Internet Service Provider (ISP): An organization that provides access to the Internet. AOL, MSN, and CompuServe are examples of paid services; Juno, BlueLight, and NetZero are examples of free ISPs.

Intranet: Like an Internet used within organizations. The network, comprised of web pages, is confined to a single organization, not necessarily a single site. Usually password protected. An intranet can be hosted by the Internet. (See pages 25–26.)

Java: A computer language especially good for the web. It can send little programs to your computer, that then run locally. The most common example are little animations that appear when some web sites are accessed.

Job board: A web site with job listings, such as www.monster.com. (See pages 95–101.)

JPEG files: A way to compress and store images. Losing only 2 percent of the information of the image (an undetectable loss to the human eye) can often result in compressing an image to 10 percent of its original size. Compressing images is highly desirable on the web, as uncompressed images take a long time to download. (See page 60.)

Keyword: A summarizing or representative word that search engines can use to find sites. (See pages 91–93.)

Knowledge economy: An economy based primarily on knowledge and information (rather than on products as is the case in industrial economies or food production as in agrarian economies). (See pages 4–5.)

Link: A way for users to move directly to another web site, as opposed to a "hyperlink," which is a way for users to move to another location within the same web site.

Listserv: Hardware and software that supports an email list, such as www.egroups.com

Lurking: Reading the postings of an electronic group without contributing to the discussion. Lurkers generally outnumber posters.

Mail merge: A feature of a word processor or other program that allows for a form letter, with fields such as name and address filled in from a database when the letters are printed. (See page 32.)

MB: Megabyte, representing 2^{20}, or approximately 1 million characters of information. Kb (kilobyte) represents 1,024 characters of information; Gb (gigabyte) represents a billion characters, and Tb (terabyte) represents a trillion characters.

Metasite: A web site that offers diversity of information, or a compendium of sources of information on a similar topic.

Metatag: An HTML command that does not display to the user, but allows search engines to help index and display information about the web page. (See pages 67–68.)

Navigation: Finding your way around systems of menus or help files. The "Navigation Bar" aids you by using clickable images with subscripts to guide you along.

Neticism: A phrase likely to be found on, or referring to, the web. An example is BTW (by the way). (See pages 46–47.)

Netiquette: Shortened form of "Internet etiquette." Conventional and responsible practices that govern polite online behavior.

Newbie: A person new to the Internet or to a discussion forum.

Newsgroup: A USENET group focused on one topic. A public forum or discussion area on a network where users can read and post messages on the BBS. (See pages 43–44.)

Password: A secret sequence of characters used to keep unauthorized users from accessing your files, computer, or network. Change your password on a regular basis and avoid using words and numbers corresponding to you.

PGP (Pretty Good Privacy): Software that protects the privacy of information transferred online. A free version of the software is at www.pgp.com. *Caution:* PGP can be export controlled, so care needs to be exercised if encrypted information is to be shared internationally.

Post: An electronic message left on an electronic bulletin board or in a chat room (noun), or to place an electronic message (verb).

.rtf. (Rich Text Format): A format for saving and sending files that eliminates some of the formatting information that may not transfer well. (See page 94.)

Real time: The equivalent of "live" for television. Can also refer to programs that run fast enough to display results as fast as they happen, or fast enough that the user sees no perceptible delays.

Search engine: Web service that searches the web for keywords. www.yahoo.com is a common example. (See pages 14–15.)

Server: Client/server network that stores files, provides printer access to individual workstations, and often provides a portal for email and the web.

SET (Secure Electronic Transaction): A standard used by Master-Card and Visa for securing online credit card transactions.

Signature: Information created by a user that is automatically appended to outgoing email and postings. Usually contains name, company, email address, or other pertinent information. Also called an automatic professional footer. (See page 39.)

Snail mail: Mail delivered by hand (e.g., the U.S. Postal Service) and is consequently slow compared to electronic methods.

Spam: Junk mail sent through email to many addresses, or to newsgroups or message forums. Generally seen as unethical since junk mail is paid for by the recipient's site and not by the sender.

SSL (Secure Socket Layer): A browser support program that protects the privacy of information transmitted. A similar privacy protection program is Secure Electronic Transfer (SET).

Streaming: To receive continuously. For example, *streaming audio* or *streaming video* is the web equivalent to radio or television. Common on sites with domain names ending in .tv.

Subscribe/unsubscribe: A way to get added to or deleted from electronic mailing lists. Often a person is added to or deleted from a list by typing the words "subscribe" or "unsubscribe" in the subject line of an email message.

Surfing: Browsing through newsgroups, the web, or other online information.

Technophobe: Person afraid of technology.

Technophyle: A computer/technology enthusiast.

Telecommuting: Working at home using technology, such as the Internet, or delivering product via the Internet. (See pages 6–7.)

Thumbnails: Small image that loads much more quickly. Clicking on a thumbnail brings up the full-sized version of the image. (See page 60.)

Upload: To send information from your local computer to a remote computer.

URL (Uniform Resource Locator): The "address" of a place on the Internet. An example is www.nameofcompany.com.

USENET: A group of thousands of newsgroups on various topics distributed on the Internet. Posting, reading, responding, and emailing can all take place. To search USENET groups, go to dejanews. (See page 44.)

Username: An identification name. Required to log onto multi-user system, BBS, or online service.

Virtual: A presence that is electronically defined, and may have no basis in reality. A company may have a "virtual storefront" via a web page.

Virtual companies: Companies that do all their customer interaction via the web and telephone, and may have no offices or stores at all. (See page 7.)

Virus: A program that copies itself, infects disks or programs, and disrupts operation of the computer.

Web (World Wide Web, WWW, or Internet): Thousands of interlinked computers containing millions of web pages. Uses hypertext. Also uses multimedia such as graphics, audio, and video to display information. You need a modem and an ISP to access it. (See pages 5–6.)

Web conferencing: Using web video and audio for a meeting. (See page 6.)

Web counter: A small program that keeps track of how many times a web page is visited. (See page 69.)

Web page: A file of information on the web seen by users as one page of information on the screen. (See pages 51–69.)

Web ring: A method for related sites to link to each other; *site A* links to *site B,* which links to *site C,* etc. www.webrings.com can help set up this feature. (See page 68.)

Web site: A specific location of one or more pages made available by computer from the web. (See page 13.)

WYSIWYG: (What You See Is What You Get), pronounced "wizeewig." When the computer screen, as the product is created, looks like the final printed product.

XML: A next generation enhancement to HTML. In XML, words, phrases, or images can be tagged. For example, "2000" could be tagged to be a year, or a price, or a stock number. This will greatly help search engines narrow in on the desired information.

If you have a question about a term not included in this dictionary, several glossary sites are available, including

- www.reverse-lookup.com/glossarit.html
- www.page-group.co.uk/content/glossary.html

BIBLIOGRAPHY

Baker, W., K. DeTienne, and K. Smart, "How *Fortune* 500 Companies Are Using Electronic Résumé Management Systems," *Business Communication Quarterly*, September 1998, 8–19.

Battey, J., "By the Numbers," *InfoWorld*, September 2000, 22.

Bovee, C., and J. Thill, "Business Communication Update." For free subscription, send an email with the following "To:" line: join-bcu@mh.databank.com. To contact Bovee and Thill, write to: bovee-thill@uia.net.

Conference Board, "Companies Profiting from Knowledge Management," Press Release 4543, March 2000. Available: www.conference-board.org.

Conference Board, "Knowledge Management Spreading Worldwide," Press Release 4485, May 1999. Available: www.conference-board.org.

DeTienne, K., and L. Jackson, "Knowledge Management: Understanding Theory and Developing Policy," *Competitiveness Review*, Vol. II (1), 2001, 1-11.

DeTienne, K., and R. Jensen, "Intranets and Business Model Innovation: Managing Knowledge in the Virtual Organization," *Knowledge Management and Business Model Innovation*, Yogesh Malhotra, Ed. Hershey, PA: Idea Group Publishing, 2001.

DeTienne, K., and S. Joshi, "An Examination of the Future Trends in Corporate Intranets," *Futures Research Quarterly*, Winter 1999, 5–15.

Drucker, P., "The Age of Social Transformation," *The Atlantic Monthly*, November 1994, 53–80. Available: www.theatlantic.com/politics/ecbig/soctrans.htm.

Glover, S., S. Liddle, and D. Prawitt, *ebusiness: Principles and Strategies for Accountants*. Upper Saddle River, NJ: Prentice Hall, 2001.

Hoefling, T., "If Telecommuting Is So Wonderful, Why Aren't More People Volunteering?" *Telecommuting Success: An Integrated Approach*, 1999.http://www/telsuccess.com/volunteering.htm.

Kilian, C., *Writing for the Web*. Bellingham: Self-Counsel Press, 1999.

Lynch, P., and S. Horton, *Web Style Guide*. New Haven, CT: Yale University Press, 1999.

Ministry of Economic Development, *What Is the Knowledge Economy?* June 2000. Available: http://www.med.govt.nz/pbt/infotech/knowledge_economy.

Munter, M., *Guide to Managerial Communication*, 5th Ed. Upper Saddle River, NJ: Prentice Hall, 2000.

Munter, M., "Meeting Technology: From Low-Tech to High-Tech." *Business Communication Quarterly*, June 1998, 80–87.

Munter, M., *How to Use PowerPoint 2000.* The Tuck School of Business, Dartmouth College, 2000.

Munter, M., P. Rogers, and J. Rymer, *Guidelines for Writing Email.* The Tuck School of Business, Dartmouth College, 2000.

Rosenfeld, L., and P. Morville, *Information Architecture for the World Wide Web: Designing Large-Scale Web Sites.* Sebastopol, CA: O'Reilly, 1998.

Schultz, H., *The Elements of Electronic Communication.* Boston: Allyn and Bacon, 2000.

Simons, T., "Multimedia or Bust?" *Presentations,* February 2000, 41–50.

Thompson, J., K. DeTienne, and K. Smart, "Privacy, E-mail, and Information Policy: Where Ethics Meets Reality," *IEEE Transactions on Professional Communication,* 1995, 158–164.

Timm, P., and J. Stead, *Communication Skills for Business and Professions.* Upper Saddle River, NJ: Prentice Hall, 1996.

Wonnacott, L., "The Speed of Business: If Your Pages Are Slow, Your Customers Will Go," *InfoWorld,* September 2000, 80.

Index